Collins

OCR GCSE

GW00362392

Design and Technology

Design and Technology

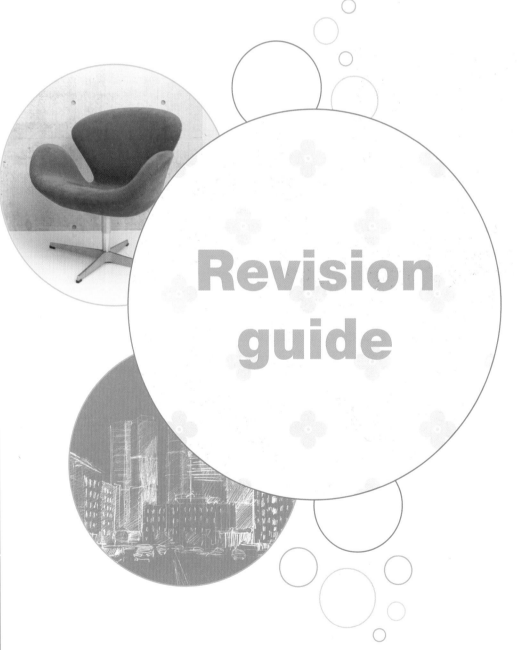

Revision guide

OCR GCSE 9-1

Revision guide

Paul Anderson and David Hills-Taylor

About this Revision Guide & Workbook

Revise

These pages provide a recap of everything you need to know for each topic.

You should read through all the information before taking the Quick Test at the end. This will test whether you can recall the key facts.

> **Quick Test**
>
> 1. What factors should be considered when exploring design contexts?
> 2. Why should designers meet with the end user and wider stakeholders?
> 3. What is a design brief and specification?

Practise

These topic-based questions appear shortly after the revision pages for each topic and will test whether you have understood the topic. If you get any of the questions wrong, make sure you read the correct answer carefully.

Review

These topic-based questions appear later in the book, allowing you to revisit the topic and test how well you have remembered the information. If you get any of the questions wrong, make sure you read the correct answer carefully.

Mix it Up

These pages feature a mix of exam-style questions for the different topics within the chapters. They will make sure you can recall the relevant information to answer a question without being told which topic it relates to.

Test Yourself on the Go

Visit our website at **collins.co.uk/collinsGCSErevision** and print off a set of flashcards. These pocket-sized cards feature questions and answers so that you can test yourself on all the key facts anytime and anywhere. You will also find lots more information about the advantages of spaced practice and how to plan for it.

Workbook

This section features even more topic-based questions as well as a practice exam paper, providing further practice opportunities for each topic to guarantee the best results.

ebook

To access the ebook revision guide visit

collins.co.uk/ebooks

and follow the step-by-step instructions.

Contents

Contents

	Revise		Practise		Review	

Technical Understanding

Manufacturing Processes and Techniques

Maths Skills in the Exam

You must be able to:

- Use maths skills to answer questions related to Design & Technology.

Some of the exam questions for GCSE Design & Technology will use skills and knowledge that have been learned in maths. The following table summarises the maths skills that might be needed. It also gives some examples of how these might be used in questions in the exam. There are lots of practice questions that include maths skills in the relevant sections of this book. Look for the maths skills logo:

Type of Maths	Skill or Knowledge	How this Might be Used
Arithmetic and Numerical Computation (M1)	Use expressions in decimal and standard form.	• Use decimal and standard form appropriately when using metric units and units of mass, length, time, money and other measures (for example 9.6×10^3 m). (Be aware that some measurements still commonly use imperial units.) • Use and apply standard form when calculating quantities of materials, cost and sizes.
	Use ratios, fractions and percentages.	• Understand and use ratios in the scaling of drawings. • Apply fractions and percentages when analysing provided tables and charts of data, survey responses and user questionnaires.  • Calculate percentages such as profit or waste savings; use percentages to compare measurements.
	Calculate surface areas and volumes (where dimensions are given).	• Calculate the surface area to determine quantities of materials. • Calculate the volume of cuboids, and simple and composite shapes.
	Apply tolerances.	• Calculate the maximum and minimum value of a quantity or size with a tolerance.
Handling Data (M2)	Diagrams, bar charts and histograms.	• Construct frequency tables, pie charts and bar charts using provided data. • Interpret the meaning of data presented in frequency tables, pie charts and bar charts. • Present data to accurately show performance over time.

Graphs (M3)	Draw and interpret graphs.	• Analyse graphs to extract information and interpret what this information shows. • Plot or draw graphs from provided data (such as performance data or responses to surveys).
	Translate information shown in graphs into numbers.	• Extract information from provided technical specifications or graphs to understand instructions or needs.
Geometry and Trigonometry (M4)	Using angular measurements in degrees: • know the basic properties of isosceles, equilateral and right-angled triangles • understand the basic rules of angular calculations and trigonometry.	• Calculate angles and dimensions in components to support marking out. • Calculate angles in structures reinforced by triangulation.
	Understand symmetry to create tessellated patterns.	• Create tessellated patterns that minimise waste of material.
	Visualise and represent 2D and 3D forms, including 2D representations of 3D objects.	• Communicate intentions to others using graphical presentation of designs. • Create accurate 2D representations from 3D objects with stated dimensions. • Interpret information to accurately present isometric drawings.
	Calculate areas of triangles and rectangles. (Note: some dimensions may not be given or need to be calculated.)	• Calculate the area to determine quantities of materials needed. • Calculate the area to determine area scale factor application.
	Calculate the surface area and volumes of cubes. (Note: some dimensions may not be given or need to be calculated.)	• Calculate the overall surface area of cuboids to determine the quantities of material needed. • Calculate the volume of cuboids to determine if an object can fit into the space. • Calculate the volume of cuboids to determine volume scale factor application.

Exploring Context and Factors Affecting the Design Process

You must be able to:

- Explain the main factors that should be considered when exploring a design context
- Write a design brief and specification for a product or system.

Exploring the Design Context

- When presented with a design context, designers will spend time exploring a range of different factors that could affect the solution that is produced.
- It is important to meet with the **end user** to speak about their requirements. These responses can then be discussed with other designers on the team.
- A spider chart is good way of recording first thoughts surrounding the context.

The 5 Ws

- The 5 Ws are a useful starting point for exploring the design context. For example:
  - **Who** – Who is the product for? Who will be the end user of the product? Who are the wider **stakeholders**? What are their requirements?
  - **What** – What are the potential solutions to the problem? What products or systems could solve the problem? What materials, components, techniques or processes could be used? What impact could it have on society and the environment?
  - **Where** – Where will the product be used? Will it be for indoor or outdoor use? Will it be in a public or private space? How could this impact on how it is designed?
  - **When** – When will the product be used? Will it be used during the day or at night? Will it be in use during busy periods of the day or when it is quieter? How could this impact on how it is designed?
  - **Why** – Why is the product being designed? Is market pull or technology push a factor?
- Designers should also consider the potential impact of cultural, moral and economic issues. For example, in Japan people often sit on the floor to eat, which affects the way furniture is designed; during a period of recession people have less money to spend, which could affect the quality of materials that are used in products.

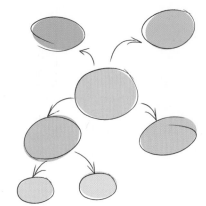

A spider chart

Japanese furniture designed for eating while sitting on the floor

Design Brief and Specification

- Once the context has been thoroughly explored, a **design brief** and design specification should be written.

Design Brief

- The design situation is usually outlined first, followed by the design brief itself.
- The design brief is a short description of the design problem and how it is to be solved.
- It is typically written as a few sentences or a short paragraph. An example is shown below:

Situation
Developing numeracy skills early in life equips young children well for when they start school. Many of these skills can be learned through play.

Brief
I am going to design and make a toy for young children aged 3–5 years. The toy must be interactive and educational to the child. It should help them to improve their numeracy skills.

Design Specification

- The design specification is a list of measurable design criteria that the product or system must meet. It is usually written as a set of bullet points.
- It provides much more detail on the specific requirements of the product or system.
- A good specification will include criteria related to cost, aesthetics, function, ergonomics, quality and the materials and components to be used. It may also consider social, environmental and sustainability requirements.

A toy designed to help build the numeracy skills of young children

> **Key Point**
>
> A design brief gives a short description of the problem that is to be solved.

Quick Test

1. What factors should be considered when exploring design contexts?
2. Why should designers meet with the end user and wider stakeholders?
3. What are a design brief and a design specification?

> **Key Words**
>
> end user
> stakeholder
> design brief

Usability

You must be able to:

- Explain the difference between inclusive and exclusive design
- Describe how ergonomics and anthropometric data are used to make products that are easy to use and interact with
- Describe the meaning of aesthetics and explain how it is used in the design of products.

Impact of Design on Lifestyle

- Design plays an important role in helping to improve people's lifestyles.
- This can include the design of products to assist those with disabilities or special requirements. For example, a phone designed with large buttons and text for older people could help them communicate better with family and loved ones.
- In developing countries, products and systems can be designed to ensure that people have an acceptable standard of living. For example, sustainably powered lighting systems may be used by people living in countries with little or no access to mains electricity.
- Designers should be mindful of any potential negative impacts of their designs on people's lifestyles. Sometimes these effects are unexpected or unintended.

A mobile phone designed with large buttons and text for older people

Ease of Use

- Designers want their products to be easy for people to use and to interact with.
- To achieve this, they consider factors such as aesthetics, **ergonomics**, anthropometrics and the inclusivity or exclusivity of their designs.

Inclusive and Exclusive Design

- **Inclusive design** is about designing products and systems that can be used by everyone. Ideally, this should be without any special adaptations.
- Everyone is different, so it is not always possible to design in a completely inclusive way. However, designers will often aim to cater for as many people as possible.
- **Exclusive design** is when products are designed for a particular group of people or a limited audience. For example, car seats are designed specifically for babies or very young children.

A car seat for babies

Key Point

Inclusive design is about ensuring that products and systems can be used by everyone, or as many people as possible.

Ergonomics and Anthropometrics

Ergonomics

- Ergonomics is about understanding how people interact with the products and systems around them (sometimes called the user interface). It is a key factor in ensuring that a product is easy to use.
- When considering ergonomics, designers will think about factors such as comfort and safety. For example, the handle of a garden tool can be designed so that it fits comfortably in the hand.

Anthropometric Data

- Anthropometrics is the study of the human body and how it moves.
- **Anthropometric data** is measurements that are taken from millions of people of different shapes and sizes and placed in charts.
- Measurements include hip height, shoulder height, head circumference and hand length.
- Designers can make use of these charts when designing products and systems. For example, when designing head gear making use of head circumference sizes can ensure the product fits the people it is intended for.
- When using anthropometric data designers will often work from the 5th to the 95th percentile. This ensures that 90% of the population is catered for.

Aesthetics

- **Aesthetics** is about how well a design appeals to the human senses. It is also often described as the appreciation of the attractiveness or beauty in a product.
- The original Apple iMac G3 computer, launched in 1998, is considered a famous example of aesthetic design. It did away with the usual beige and grey rectangular designs of the time and instead made use of bright, translucent colours and curved shapes. It was a huge commercial success.

> **Key Point**
>
> Ergonomics and anthropometrics are used to ensure that products are easy to use and interact with.

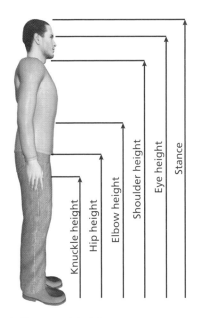

Anthropometric data

The Apple iMac G3

> **Quick Test**
>
> 1. What is meant by the term 'inclusive design'?
> 2. What is anthropometric data and how is it used in the design of products and systems?
> 3. What is aesthetics?

> **Key Words**
>
> ergonomics
> inclusive design
> exclusive design
> anthropometric data

Exploring Existing Designs

You must be able to:

- Explain the reasons for exploring existing designs
- Understand the factors to consider when exploring existing designs.

Reasons for Exploring Existing Designs

- Exploring existing designs is a very important part of the design process. It involves analysing and critiquing a design, product or system that has already been produced.
- Completing this task helps designers to learn from the successes and failures of the past. It gives them inspiration and ideas for new products and systems.

Factors to Consider When Exploring Existing Designs

- There are a number of factors to consider when exploring existing designs. Analysing how each of these has been used in the design of a product or system gives a complete picture of its overall effectiveness.
- The materials, components and processes that have been used:
  - The materials and components used have a direct influence on how well a product or system functions.
  - For example, a product that is to be used outdoors would have to make use of materials that are resistant to weather damage. A system that needs to check changes in light level would need to use a suitable light sensor.
  - The processes used to make the product should also be appropriate for its intended use.
- The influence of fashion, trends, taste and style:
  - Product designs are often influenced by what is 'in fashion' at the time. For example, clothing designs.
  - This changes continuously and designers need to keep on top of current trends if they are to continue to produce popular products.
- The influence of marketing and branding:
  - Companies use branding and marketing to promote and advertise their products to the wider public.
  - For example, a good logo will allow the product and/or company to be instantly recognisable.
  - Adverts on the internet, TV, radio and billboards can also be used to promote the product.

> **Key Point**
>
> Exploring existing designs helps designers to learn from the successes and failures of the past.

The Volkswagen car logo is instantly recognisable

- The impact on usability:
  - It is very important that a product is easy to use, inclusively designed and aesthetically pleasing.
  - Where appropriate the designer should make use of anthropometric data and ergonomics to ensure that the product is comfortable to use.
- The impact on society and the environment:
  - It should be considered how the product has or could impact on the environment and wider society.
  - For example, has it been made from recycled or recyclable materials? Can it be disposed of in a sustainable manner? Have there been any unintended consequences for different groups of people or the wider public?
  - Life cycle assessment is a tool for systematically evaluating the environmental aspects of a product or system.
- The work of past and present professionals and companies:
  - Designers over the years have produced a wide range of different products and systems that can be learned from.
  - Some designs are now considered as design classics due to the influence that they have had.
  - For example, Philippe Starck's Juicy Salif lemon squeezer is well known for its distinct form, but often criticised for being impractical to use. However, it remains very popular.
  - However, not all designs have been successful. For example, in 1985 the Sinclair C5 electric vehicle was launched to much expectation, but was ultimately a commercial flop.

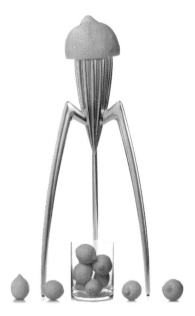

Philippe Starck's Juicy Salif lemon squeezer

The Sinclair C5 electric vehicle

Quick Test

1. Why do designers explore existing designs, products and systems?
2. What are the main factors to consider when exploring existing designs?
3. What is 'life cycle assessment'?
4. What can designers learn from failed products?

Key Words

exploring existing designs
function
marketing
life cycle assessment
design classic

New and Emerging Technologies

You must be able to:

- Analyse and evaluate the influence that new and emerging technologies have on design decisions
- Explain the impacts of new and emerging technologies on industry, society and the environment.

Influence on Design Decisions

- Designers should be able to critically evaluate how **new and emerging technologies** influence design choices.
- As part of this they should consider potential future scenarios from different perspectives.

Ethics

- Just because a new technology can be used, it does not mean that it should be used. New technologies are constantly being developed, but designers must consider their ethical implications.
- For example, **nanotechnology** could have a huge impact on how healthcare is provided in the future. However, some people think that we should not be placing artificial components into the human body.

The Environment

- New technologies can be used to produce more environmentally friendly and sustainable designs.
- For example, public buses are being introduced in China that have electric engines powered by super capacitors. These are estimated to just use one tenth of the energy of a diesel-powered bus.
- Another example is the development of **bioplastics**. These reduce the need to drill for the oil that is used to produce standard plastics. Disposable carrier bags are being designed to be biodegradable, which means less waste will be sent to landfill sites.

Product Enhancement

- Product enhancement is any change that makes a product better in some way.
- New materials or manufacturing technologies often result in the improvement of products or the development of new ones.
- One example is the use of **smart materials** such as quantum tunnelling composite (QTC). This is a flexible polymer that becomes a conductor of electricity when squeezed. This has allowed the creation of membrane switches for use in mobile phones. It also has many potential future uses in e-textiles.

Nanotechnology could have a huge impact on healthcare in the future

Key Point

Designers should be able to critically evaluate the influence of new and emerging technologies on design choices.

Electric bus, China

Impacts when Designing Solutions

- New and emerging technologies impact on the design of solutions to problems.
- Designers should be able to explore these impacts within different industrial, social and environmental contexts.

Industry and Enterprise: The Circular Economy

- The design industry typically operates using a linear model. Products are made, used and then disposed of at the end of their life. This has many problems, such as heavy reliance on fossil fuels and the creation of unsustainable amounts of landfill waste.
- The **circular economy** has the potential to radically change how products are designed and manufactured. It is a model that aims to increase the use of renewable energy and design products that are 'made to be made again'.
- For example, products could be designed that can be easily disassembled, so that the main components can be reused in new products.

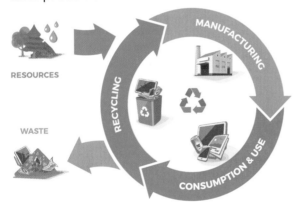

The circular economy

People and the Environment

- New technologies can have a huge impact on lifestyle, culture, society and the environment.
- For example, developments in communications technology mean that people are now able to keep in touch with each other in countless different ways, wherever there is wireless network access. This has completely changed how society operates in the developed world.
- Another example is technology that can read eye movements and turn them into speech. This could drastically improve the lifestyles of people who are otherwise unable to speak by almost literally 'reading their mind'.

Key Words

new and emerging
  technologies
nanotechnology
bioplastics
smart materials
circular economy

Quick Test

1. What is product enhancement?
2. What is the circular economy?
3. How can new technologies impact on society?

Sources of Energy

You must be able to:

- Describe how energy is generated, transferred and stored
- Explain the appropriate use of renewable and non-renewable energy sources to power products and systems.

Non-Renewable Energy Sources

- **Non-renewable energy sources** are sources that will eventually run out. The main examples are fossil fuels and nuclear fuel.

Fossil Fuels

- **Fossil fuels** are formed from the remains of dead organisms over a very long period of time. Examples are coal, oil and natural gas.
- Fossil fuels are burned to create steam. This then turns turbines, which drive the generators that produce electricity.
- Burning fossil fuels releases carbon dioxide into the atmosphere, which can contribute to global warming.
- Fossil fuels will eventually run out.

Nuclear Fuel

- The steam needed to turn turbines and hence drive the generators is created using a nuclear reactor.
- Nuclear fission controls the reactor heat. This requires uranium, which is finite.
- Making greater use of **nuclear energy** means there is less need for fossil fuels.
- Although accidents are rare they can result in radioactive material being released into the environment. This can cause serious health problems for people living nearby.
- Strict procedures for disposal and storage of waste must be followed, as nuclear materials can stay hazardous for thousands of years.

Cooling towers at a nuclear power plant

Renewable Energy Sources

- **Renewable energy sources** are sustainable and will not run out. They are sources that can replenish themselves quickly. Examples include wind, hydro, tidal and solar power. Agricultural crops can also be used to create biofuels.

Solar

- Photovoltaic cells, or solar panels, make use of **solar energy** by collecting and converting light from the sun into an electric current.
- Sunlight will not run out for billions of years, so there is an almost endless supply available.
- No waste products or greenhouse gases are emitted.

 Key Point

Renewable energy sources can replenish themselves quickly and so will not run out.

Solar panels producing electricity for a house

- Solar panels will produce less electricity when there is less sunlight. They produce no electricity at night.
- Installation and maintenance costs can be high.

Wind

- Turbines that drive the generators are turned by the wind.
- The amount of electricity that is produced by wind energy depends on how much wind there is, so where they are positioned is crucial.
- No waste products or greenhouse gases are emitted.
- Some people feel that wind turbines are too noisy and do not like how they impact on the look of the local landscape.

Hydro

- To harness hydro energy water is held in a reservoir and behind a dam. It is then released, turning a turbine which then generates electricity.
- Although clean and sustainable, creating a reservoir involves flooding large areas of land. This destroys habitats and forces people to move to new homes.
- Tidal is a form of hydropower that harnesses the energy from the tides of the sea to generate electricity.

Transferring Energy

- Once energy has been generated it must be transferred to its place of use.
- Electricity is transmitted from power stations to homes and buildings via the National Grid.
- The electricity is transmitted through cables at high voltage to minimise energy losses via heat. As high voltages are very dangerous, this requires the cables to be placed on pylons out of the reach of people and animals.
- Step-up transformers are used to increase the voltage to the required levels for transmission. Step-down transformers reduce it back down to the level that we use in our homes.

Storing Energy

- Sometimes energy will not be used straightaway and must therefore be stored until it is needed.
- Batteries, super capacitors and fuel cells are all methods of achieving this.

Wind turbines

Electricity transmission pylons

A pair of 1.5V AA batteries

> **Key Point**
>
> Energy can be stored using batteries, super capacitors and fuel cells.

> **Key Words**
>
> non-renewable energy source
> fossil fuel
> nuclear energy
> renewable energy source
> solar energy
> wind energy
> hydro energy

> **Quick Test**
>
> 1. How is electricity generated using fossil fuels?
> 2. What are the main sources of renewable energy?
> 3. What are the advantages of using renewable sources of energy to power products?
> 4. Why is electricity transmitted at high voltages across the National Grid?

Wider Influences on Designing and Making

You must be able to:

* Explain how designing and making is affected by environmental, social and ethical issues
* Discuss the benefits of fair trade for producers and consumers.

Environmental Issues and Initiatives

* Products can impact on the environment at all stages of their life cycle, from sourcing materials all the way to disposal of the product once it is no longer useful. Designers must be mindful of this and take steps to reduce these effects.
* The 6 Rs of sustainability is a tool widely used to help designers reduce the impact of their products on the environment. It can be used as a checklist for each product that is designed.
    - **Reduce** – How can the amount of materials and components used in the product be reduced? Is the product itself necessary?
    - **Rethink** – How can the design of the product be changed so that it is less harmful to the environment? Can a better way to solve the problem be found?
    - **Refuse** – Should the product be produced if it is not sustainably designed? Is the packaging necessary or can it be removed?
    - **Recycle** – Is the product made using recycled materials? Could the materials be recycled once the product is no longer useful?
    - **Reuse** – Could the product be used in a different way once its current use has expired? Could it be disassembled so that its materials and components could be reused in other products?
    - **Repair** – Is the product easy to repair? Are replacement components readily available in case of failure?
* There is a range of wider initiatives designed to help to improve the sustainability of products and reduce their impact on the environment. Examples of these include:
    - Internationally agreed symbols on product packaging inform consumers about the sustainability of products. For example:
        - the Mobius Loop shows that a product can be recycled.
        - the Green Dot symbol indicates that the manufacturer contributes to the cost of recycling.
    - In 2015, to try and reduce their use, the UK government introduced a 5p levy for every plastic carrier bag purchased at a large store. These bags are non-recyclable and can cause damage to wildlife.

Key Point

The 6 Rs can be used to help designers evaluate the impact of their products on the environment.

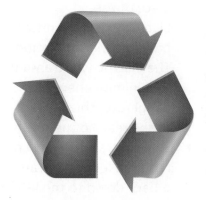

The Mobius Loop symbol shows that a product can be recycled

The Green Dot symbol indicates the manufacturer contributes to the cost of recycling

- The United Nations has produced a set of global sustainable development goals. These include aims to end hunger, reduce inequality and provide access to clean energy for all.
- Manufacturers are making greater use of biodegradable materials in the design of their products and packaging.

Fair Trade

- Fair trade is a movement that works to help people in developing countries get a fair deal for the products that they produce.
- Producers are paid an agreed minimum rate for many products. This gets paid even if global prices fall.
- They also receive a Fairtrade Premium payment that they can use to invest in areas such as local education and healthcare.
- Many consumers like to buy fair trade products as it fits with their values and principles.
- The Fairtrade Certification Mark shows that a product meets fair trade standards.

The Fairtrade Mark placed on imported bananas

Social and Ethical Awareness

- Products can also have effects on wider society. These can be both positive and negative. Sometimes these effects are unexpected or unintended.
  - For example, mobile smartphones have completely changed how people communicate with each other in the last decade.
- Just because a product can be produced does not automatically mean that it should be. Designers should consider whether an idea is an ethical design.
  - For example, research is currently being conducted on the 3D printing of human organs. Some believe this could solve current organ donation problems, but others argue that it would be unethical.

Smartphones have completely changed how people communicate with each other

Key Point

Designs can have consequences for wider society. Sometimes these are unintended or unexpected.

Quick Test

1. What are the 6 Rs of sustainability?
2. What are the main benefits of fair trade for producers of products?
3. Why is it important that designers consider the potential impact of products on society?

Key Words

recycle
sustainable development
biodegradable material
fair trade
ethical design

Viability of Design Solutions

You must be able to:

- Discuss the importance of commercial viability and marketability of a product or system
- Explain how the needs of end users and stakeholders affect product viability
- Calculate the quantities and sizes of materials and components to be used in a product or system.

Ensuring a Product is Viable

- **Viability** is when a product is not only purchased initially, but performs well enough for it to be recommended to others, and for sales to continue.
- A product's viability can be assessed in terms of potential **commercial impact**, its marketability and its ability to meet the needs of users and stakeholders.
- Checking whether a design is potentially viable ensures that valuable time and money is not wasted on a product that will not be successful.
- If a design is found to not be potentially viable it can be refined, redesigned or even abandoned completely.

Commercial Viability and Marketability

- Products designed and manufactured commercially are intended to be sold to make a profit. A company will eventually go out of business if it is constantly making a loss on its sales.
- It must be considered whether there is a potential market for a new product. This can be done through market research, or by analysing the success of similar products produced by competitors.
- Often the first product of its type to take advantage of an identified market is the most commercially successful, which can have a huge impact on the company responsible for it. One famous example of this was the race between Motorola and the telecoms giant AT&T to create the first mobile phone. Motorola's success in 1973 propelled them from being a small company into the position of market leaders. This was a position that they held for over two decades.
- Conversely, even the best company marketing departments will struggle to successfully advertise and promote a product for which there is little or no market.
- The cost of materials, components and manufacture must also be factored in when deciding whether a design is commercially viable. The more a product costs to produce, the higher its selling price will need to be to recover those costs. If this

Motorola produced the first working mobile phone in 1973, resulting in them becoming market leaders for over two decades

Key Point

New products must have a potential market open to them if they are to be commercially viable.

becomes too high the product will no longer be viable, as few consumers will want to purchase it.

Meeting User and Stakeholder Requirements

- For a product or system to be viable it should meet the needs of end users and stakeholders.
- If a product does not meet the needs of end users then sales will be poor. Worse still, competitors producing a better product may take business away from the company.
- Some products are exceptionally good at meeting user needs and so sales continue to grow a long time after they are first released. For example, the Apple iPod is over 15 years old yet continues to be the market leader in portable music players.
- If stakeholders do not feel that a product or system being designed is viable, they may withdraw their support or funding for it. This could lead to financial difficulties for the company.

The Apple iPod has experienced strong sales for over 15 years

Calculating Costs

- Designers must be able to calculate the quantities and sizes of materials and components to be used for a product.
- This can involve the use of basic fractions. For example, if one quarter of the length of a piece of softwood is 40 mm, then the total length of the piece of softwood would be 160 mm.
- A **bill of materials** can be produced using spreadsheet software that lists all the materials and components needed, along with their costs to purchase. A formula can then be entered which calculates the total cost. One benefit of this is that if the cost of one or more materials changes the figures on the spreadsheet can be altered and the new total cost of materials calculated automatically.

Key Point

Stakeholders may withdraw funding or support for a product if they do not think it is viable.

A designer using spreadsheet software to calculate material costs

Quick Test

1. What factors should be considered when assessing the commercial viability of a product?
2. What is meant by the term 'marketability'?
3. Why must the needs of stakeholders be considered when assessing viability?

Key Words

viability
commercial impact
bill of materials

Practice Questions

Design Considerations

1 **a)** Define the term 'stakeholder'.

....

....

.... [2]

b) Explain why it is important that the opinions of stakeholders are considered when exploring a design context.

....

....

....

....

.... [3]

c) Explain how economic factors can influence the design of a product.

....

....

....

....

.... [3]

2 **a)** Explain the advantages and disadvantages of making greater use of renewable energy sources to power products and systems.

[6]

b) Give **two** factors that should be considered when designing a user interface for a product.

1.

2. [2]

c) Give **two** examples of new and emerging technologies.

1.

2. [2]

3 **a)** Describe **three** considerations that should be taken account of when exploring existing designs.

1.

2.

3.

[6]

b) Give **two** factors that affect the viability of a product.

1. ....

2. .... [2]

4 **a)** Explain **two** benefits of fair trade to producers of products.

1. ....

....

....

....

2. ....

....

....

.... [4]

b) Explain **one** reason why a consumer might choose **not** to buy a fair trade product.

....

....

.... [2]

c) Define the term 'global sustainable development'.

....

....

.... [2]

5   Name each of these logos and explain what they mean.

a)

_____

_____ [2]

b)

_____

_____ [2]

6   What are the 6 Rs? Tick the correct options.

Rearrange	☐	Repair	☐
Reuse	☐	Refuse	☐
Reduce	☐	Reintroduce	☐
Rewrite	☐	Renew	☐
Rotate	☐	Recycle	☐
Rethink	☐	Reinforce	☐

[6]

7   Describe the difference between inclusive design and exclusive design.

_____

_____

_____

_____ [2]

Total Marks _____ / 46

Graphical Techniques 1

You must be able to:

- Create freehand 2D and 3D sketches
- Annotate sketches to explain design decisions and show links to the specification.

Sketching

- Freehand sketching is a quick method of creating and communicating design ideas.
- Freehand sketches do not have to follow conventions. For example, they don't need to be to scale or include exact details.
- 2D sketches are often used to convey information, such as providing more detail about a feature on an associated 3D sketch.

2D sketches of packaging

3D Sketching

- 3D sketches can be produced freehand, by using crating or by isometric projection.
- Crating involves drawing a feint box around the object to be drawn. This can be used to provide guidelines for the drawing or to draw between outlines mirrored on different faces.
- Isometric projection can be used to produce a 3D object to scale. It uses lines at 30° to the baseline (60° to the edges). Isometric paper has a grid which can be used as a guide.
- Sketches can be rendered to make them more realistic. This means adding colour, tone or texture.
- Tone can be created by using shading to show areas of light and shadow.

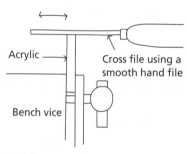

2D information sketch

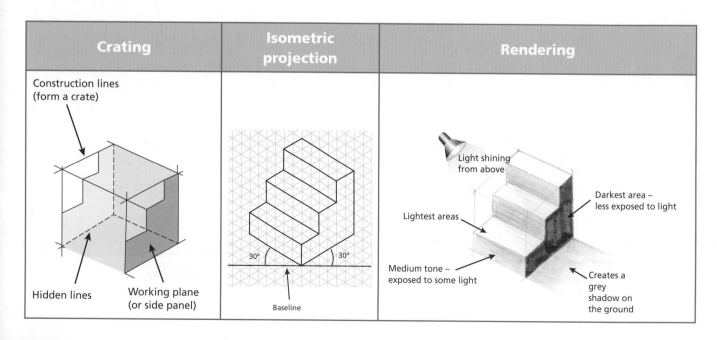

Crating	Isometric projection	Rendering
Construction lines (form a crate) Hidden lines Working plane (or side panel)	30° 30° Baseline	Light shining from above Lightest areas Medium tone – exposed to some light Darkest area – less exposed to light Creates a grey shadow on the ground

Annotation

- **Annotation** means adding notes and labels to drawings and sketches.
- These should not just be descriptive; for example, colours or materials. They should explain the design decisions and link the features of the design to the specification.
- Examples of sentence starters for good annotation include:
    - *This meets/doesn't meet my design specification requirements because …*
    - *The colours and finishes I would use are … and would be applied by …*
    - *This would cost less if …*
    - *To make sure this is safe I would have to …*
    - *This could be made from … because …*
    - *The processes used to make this feature would be … because …*
    - *This is easy /difficult to make because …*
    - *This design was inspired by …*
    - *I like/don't like this design because ….*

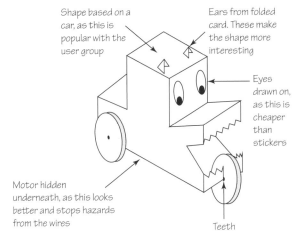

Annotated sketch for a novelty toy vehicle

> **Key Point**
>
> Sketches are a quick method to create and communicate design ideas.

> **Key Point**
>
> Good annotation is essential to explain design features and show they link to your design specification.

Sketch Modelling

- **Sketch modelling** is the process of creating a 3D sketch from a 2D shape using **CAD** software.
- The 2D shape could be a scanned drawing, or could be drawn directly into the software using a drawing tablet or mouse.

> **Key Words**
>
> scale
> crating
> isometric projection
> rendering
> annotation
> sketch modelling
> CAD

> **Quick Test**
>
> 1. Name three methods used to produce 3D sketches.
> 2. What angle to the baseline are the lines on an isometric projection?
> 3. What is the purpose of rendering a sketch?

Graphical Techniques 2

You must be able to:

- Describe how to produce an exploded drawing
- Describe how mathematical modelling is used to communicate design ideas
- Explain how flow charts are used and how to produce a flow chart.

Exploded Drawings

- **Exploded drawings** (also known as exploded views) show how the parts of a product fit together.
- The parts should be lined up and the correct size relative to the other parts.
- They are especially useful to people who are assembling products made from lots of different parts. They are often included, for example, in the instructions for furniture that the user has to put together themselves.

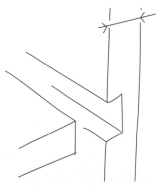

Simple exploded view of a joint

Exploded drawing of a laptop	Exploded drawing of a pencil sharpener	Exploded drawing of an LED lightbulb
	Screw fitting — Blade — Case — 30° 30° Baseline	

Mathematical Modelling

- A **mathematical model** is a way of simulating real-life situations using mathematical formulae.
- Mathematical models can be used to demonstrate how a product or system works, how a system will change if it is modified or how a product should be designed for optimum performance.
- Computer simulations are normally mathematical models.
- Most models are carried out using computer software, as they involve quite complicated formulae and many calculations.

> **Key Point**
>
> Exploded drawings show how the parts of a product fit together.

- Uses range from calculating the values of components to use in an electrical circuit to designing the shape of speedboat hulls, determining how strong a bridge needs to be and simulating the testing of aircraft in wind tunnels.

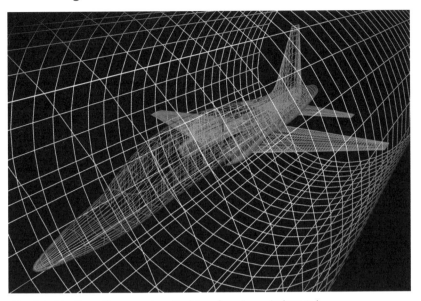

Simulated testing of how an aircraft will perform in a wind tunnel

Flow Charts

- Flow charts show the order in which a series of commands or events are carried out.
- Each type of command is represented by a different symbol. These are linked together by arrows to show the correct sequence of events.
  - Terminators represent the start and end of a process.
  - Decisions are choices that need to be made. They determine what happens next.
  - Process boxes are instructions or actions.
  - Inputs/outputs show things added to, or taken away from, the process.
- Flow charts can be used to program microcontrollers or to represent the sequence of operations needed to make a product.

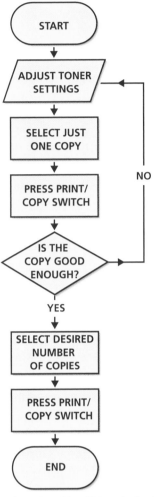

Flow chart identifying the basic process of making several copies using a photocopier

Terminator	Decision	Process	Input/Output

Flow chart symbols

> **Key Point**
>
> Flow charts show the sequence in which a series of commands is carried out.

Quick Test

1. What is the purpose of an exploded view?
2. Give two examples of how mathematical models are used.
3. Which symbol represents a decision on a flow chart?

> **Key Words**
>
> exploded drawing
> mathematical model
> flow chart

Approaches to Designing

You must be able to:

- Describe the main features of iterative design, user-centred design and a systems-based approach to design
- Explain the advantages and disadvantages of each design approach.

Different Design Approaches

- Design approaches are philosophies that guide how the design process takes place.
- Three of the most widely used design approaches are iterative design, user-centred design and a systems-based approach.
- Each approach has its own advantages and disadvantages that should be considered before it is put into practice.

Iterative Design

- Iterative design is a cyclic approach.
- Each iteration of design is tested and evaluated. Changes and refinements are then made, leading to a new iteration.
- Dyson vacuum cleaners are good examples of products designed using an iterative process. The original DC01 was developed as a result of thousands of different prototypes.
- Advantages of iterative design:
  - Because each iteration is fully tested and evaluated it is more likely that problems with the design will be discovered and dealt with earlier.
  - It encourages focus on the most critical aspects of a product's design.
  - User feedback is constantly being gathered.
  - Evidence of progress of the design of the product can be easily provided to stakeholders.
- Disadvantages of iterative design:
  - Designers can be so focused on the current iteration that they sometimes lose sight of the bigger design picture.
  - It can be time consuming if a lot of prototypes or iterations need to be produced.

User-Centred Design

- User-centred design is an approach where the needs and wants of the end user are considered extensively at each stage of the design process.
- Advantages of user-centred design:
  - The end user feels that they are being listened to and so has a greater sense of ownership of the final product.
  - Listening to the end user at each design stage means it is more likely that the final product will meet their expectations.

> **Key Point**
>
> Using an iterative design approach makes it more likely that problems with the design will be discovered earlier in the process.

Dyson make use of an iterative process when designing products

- Disadvantages of user-centred design:
  - It requires extra time to meet and hold discussions with the user, and to alter the design as a result of the user's feedback.
  - If the design becomes too focused on a particular end user's requirements, it may become unviable to sell to the wider public.

Systems Thinking

- The systems-based approach is often used when designing electronic, mechanical and mechatronic systems.
- It is a top-down approach that starts with an overview of the overall system in terms of its input, process and output sub-systems. The details of the individual components of each sub-system are then considered later.
- Advantages of a systems approach:
  - It does not require highly specialist knowledge of electronic or mechanical components to design the overview of the system.
  - The top-down approach makes it easy to communicate how the system will work to non-technical specialists, such as clients and stakeholders.
  - The system is designed in blocks, so it is easier to find errors or faults in the design.
- Disadvantages of a systems approach:
  - Because of the block-based design approach, it can lead to the use of components that are not necessary.
  - If unnecessary components are used it can lead to larger systems and extra cost.

Key Point

User-centred design considers the needs and wants of the end user at each stage of the design process.

Many electronic systems are designed using a systems-based approach

Quick Test

1. What is iterative design?
2. What are the advantages of user-centred design?
3. When is the systems-based approach often used?

Key Words

iterative design
user-centred design
systems-based approach

Review Questions

Design Considerations

1 **a)** Explain how new and emerging technologies impact on the development of design solutions.

....

....

....

....

....

....

....

....

....

....

.... **[6]**

b) Give **one** factor that should be considered when exploring existing designs.

....

.... **[1]**

c) Give **one** factor that should be considered when exploring the design context.

....

.... **[1]**

2 **a)** Define the term 'inclusive design'.

....

.... [1]

b) What is anthropometric data?

....

....

.... [2]

c) A designer is creating an idea for a new helmet for firefighters. Explain how anthropometric data could be used to help the designer.

....

....

....

....

....

.... [3]

d) Give **one** reason why marketability should be considered when considering the viability of a product.

....

.... [1]

3 The 5 Ws are a useful starting point for exploring the design context. What are the 5 Ws?

....

....

....   [5]

Review Questions

4 This question is about sources of energy.

a) Give **two** examples of non-renewable energy sources.

1. ....

2. .... **[2]**

b) Wind is an example of a renewable energy source.

Give **two other** examples of renewable energy sources.

1. ....

2. .... **[2]**

c) Explain **one** advantage and **one** disadvantage of using wind energy to power products.

Advantage ....

....

....

....

Disadvantage ....

....

....

.... **[4]**

5 **a)** Define the term 'ethical design'.

....

....

.... [2]

b) Explain **three** ways that designers can ensure that their products are sustainable.

1. ....

....

....

2. ....

....

....

3. ....

....

.... [6]

Total Marks .... / 36

Practice Questions

Communicating Design Ideas

1. Describe how sketch modelling is carried out.

    ....

    ....

    ....

    ....

    ....

    ....

    .... [4]

2. Describe how mathematical modelling is used in the design process. Use examples to support your answer.

    ....

    ....

    ....

    ....

    ....

    ....

    ....

    ....

    ....

    ....

    .... [6]

3 Explain **one** benefit of **each** of the following approaches to designing.

Iterative design ....

....

....

....

User-centred design ....

....

....

....

Systems-based approach ....

....

....

....

[6]

4 Figure 1 shows a 3D sketch. What type of sketch is it?

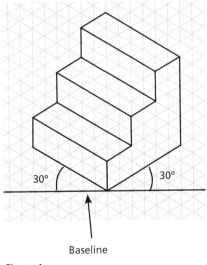

Figure 1

.... **[1]**

| **Total Marks** | / 17 |

Properties of Materials

You must be able to:

- Explain the meanings of the properties of materials
- Describe the typical properties of different types of material.

Mechanical Properties

- The mechanical properties of a material are those that involve how the materials react to some form of applied force.
- **Strength** is the ability of a material to withstand a force that is applied to it. Tensile strength resists a force that pulls the material; compressive strength resists a force that squeezes a material.
- **Hardness** is the ability of a material to resist wear or being scratched.
- Impact resistance is also known as **toughness**. This is the ability of a material to not break when a force is applied to it suddenly.
- **Corrosion resistance** is the ability of a material to resist being damaged by its environment. This might include water or chemicals.

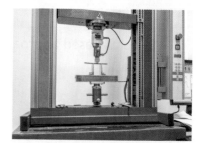

Tensile testing machine

Samples of steel after tensile testing

Physical Properties

- A physical property is a measurable characteristic of a material.
- **Density** is the mass of material per unit volume. This can be measured in kg m^{-3} or g cm^{-3}.
- Strength to weight ratio is the strength of a material divided by its density. A high strength to weight ratio means that a material is both strong and light. This is important when, for example, selecting materials to build aeroplanes.
- **Thermal conductivity** is the ability of heat to pass through a material. It is measured in watts per metre per Kelvin (W m^{-1} K^{-1}).
- **Electrical conductivity** is the ability of electricity to pass through a material. A material with low electrical conductivity has high resistance.

Hardness testing machine

Other Descriptive Terms

- **Durability** means the ability of a material to last a long time without being damaged.
- **Elasticity** is the ability of a material to return to its original shape when a force on it is removed.
- **Plasticity** is the ability of a material to be shaped or moulded. When a force is applied that changes the shape of a material, if plastic deformation occurs the material will stay in its new shape even when the force is removed.
- **Stiffness** is how rigid an object is. This is how well it can resist deformation, such as bending or buckling. Stiffness can come from the strength of the material and the shape of the object.
- **Flammability** is how easily a material burns.
- **Absorbency** is the ability of a material to draw in moisture, light or heat.

Typical Relative Properties of Different Types of Material

- The chart compares the properties of different types of material. This gives an indication of typical properties: specific named materials might have properties different to those stated.

Property	Wood	Metals	Thermopolymers
Tensile strength	Low	High	Low to medium
Compressive strength	Medium	High	Low to medium
Hardness	Low to medium	High	Low to medium
Impact resistance	Medium	High	Low to medium
Elasticity	Low	Medium to high	Low
Plasticity	Low	Medium	High
Corrosion resistance	Low	Low to medium	High
Density	Low to medium	Medium to High	Low to medium
Thermal conductivity	Low	High	Low
Electrical conductivity	Low	High	Low

FLAMMABLE
Hazard pictogram for flammable

Key Point

Types of material have different combinations of characteristic properties.

Key Words

strength
hardness
toughness
corrosion resistance
density
thermal conductivity
electrical conductivity
durability
elasticity
plasticity
stiffness
flammability
absorbency

Quick Test

1. Explain the difference between tensile and compressive strength.
2. Name four physical properties of a material (or materials).
3. Explain the difference between plasticity and elasticity.

Factors Influencing Material Selection

You must be able to:

- Describe a wide range of factors that can influence the choice of material for a product
- Explain how environmental considerations and the availability of stock forms influence material selection.

Functionality

- The material must have **functionality**, which means the mechanical and physical properties to meet the purpose that the product was designed for.
- In addition, designers and customers may have other requirements that the products must meet. These may include the following types of consideration:
  - aesthetic
  - cost
  - environmental
  - social
  - cultural
  - ethical.

> ### Key Point
>
> Selecting which material to use is not just about the material properties: there are other things to consider as well.

Aesthetic Considerations

- **Aesthetics** is how an object appeals to the five senses.
- Visual properties include colour, shape and visible texture.
- Tactile properties include the surface texture: whether the material is rough or smooth to touch, hard or soft.
- Aural properties relate to the sound made by the material. For example, the same shape of bell will make a different sound if made from metal, wood or glass.
- Smell and taste can also influence the choice of materials for products such as toys that young children may put in their mouth, disposable cutlery or clothing.

Availability of Stock Forms

- Most materials are commonly available in standard **stock forms**. If an irregular shape or size is required, this can greatly increase the cost of the material.
- The total cost of a product includes both the cost of the material and the cost to machine it into the final product.
- Machined products are often made by cutting away material. The closer the size of the available stock form to the end product, the less machining that is required. This means less waste and lower machining costs.

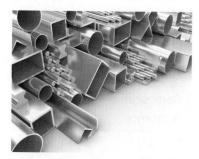

Metals are available in a wide variety of shapes and sizes

Cutting metal from a standard bar to make a product

Environmental Considerations

- Environmental considerations may be important for moral reasons or due to customer pressure.
- Renewable materials are naturally replenished; for example, wood from managed forests, or cotton.
- Non-sustainable materials use finite resources that cannot easily be replaced. For example, most synthetic plastics are made from oil.
- The environment can be damaged by the action needed to obtain the material. For example, many metal ores are obtained by quarrying, and polluting spills can occur when transporting oil.
- Consideration may also be given to what happens to the product at the end of its usable life. If the material can be recycled or reused the need to obtain more new material may be limited. If the material must go to landfill disposal it may be a potential source of pollution or endanger local habitats.

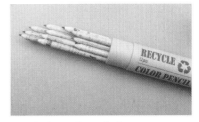

Recycled pencils made from newspaper

Social, Cultural and Ethical Considerations

- Social and cultural considerations can include:
  - Fashion: customers may want a certain style or popular aesthetic requirement that can only be achieved using a specific material. For example, they may want fabric that drapes in a certain way or furniture that looks as though it is made from a quality wood.
  - Customer preferences for buying material manufactured in some countries or not using material sources from certain countries for political reasons.
- Ethical considerations include whether workers involved in production are treated in a fair way.

The recycled symbol

Piles of waste at a city landfill

Quick Test

1. Name six types of need that a material may have to satisfy.
2. State the five aesthetic considerations.
3. Give an example of an ethical consideration that can influence the choice of material for a product.

Key Words

functionality
aesthetics
stock form

Paper and Board

You must be able to:

- Describe the characteristics and common uses of a variety of papers and boards
- Describe the standard sizes of paper
- Explain how paper and boards are converted into usable material
- Explain what happens to paper and boards at the end of their usable life.

Types of Paper and Board

Type	Characteristics	Typical Use
Layout and tracing paper	Hard and translucent Typically 50–90 gsm	Working drawings, tracing
Cartridge paper	Tough and lightly textured Typically a very light cream colour 100–150 gsm	Drawing and painting
Bleached card	Strong, high-quality, white board Made from pure bleached wood pulp 200–400 gsm	Excellent for printing; book covers, expensive packaging
Carton board (duplex board)	White surfaces with grey fibres between Tough and lightly textured Lower cost than fully bleached card 230–420 gsm	Food packaging
Corrugated cardboard	Contains two or more layers of card with interlacing fluted inner section (adds strength without a significant weight increase) Often made from recycled material, low cost From 250 gsm upwards	General-purpose material for boxes and packaging
Foil-lined board	Made by laminating aluminium foil to one side of cardboard, solid white board or duplex board Insulating properties, can keep moisture in/out	Drinks cartons, ready-meal lids
Foam board	Paper surfaces covering polystyrene centre Typically 1.5–12 mm thick	Mounting of pictures, architectural models
Expanded polystyrene (Styrofoam)	Expanded polystyrene foam containing 98% air Lightweight, easy to cut and shape, insulating properties From 5 mm thick upwards	Model making
Polypropylene sheet	Thermoplastic polymer Low density, tough, flexible and water resistant From 30 µm (micrometres) thick upwards	Packaging and labelling

Standard Sizes and Forms

- Paper comes in standard sizes, specified by an ISO (International Organization for Standardization) standard.
- A6 paper is the smallest size, measuring 105 × 148 mm; the area doubles with each size, up to A0 at 841 × 1189 mm.
- The weight of paper and card is specified in grams per square metre, referred to as gsm. In general, the higher the value of the gsm, the thicker the paper.
- Standard printer paper is generally around 80 gsm. Typically, card products are 200 gsm or more.

Source and Disposal

- Paper and card are made from wood pulp. Chemicals are added to produce the required texture and surface finish.
- Wood pulp can be sourced from managed forests, where new trees are planted to replace those that are used. This helps to reduce the environmental impact.
- Most paper and card can be recycled at the end of its life by being processed and mixed with wood pulp. However, recycled paper cannot be used to make food packaging. If put in landfill, paper will biodegrade.
- Foil-lined board is a composite material and cannot be recycled.
- Foam board, expanded polystyrene and polypropylene sheet are made from oil, a non-sustainable resource. These products are not recyclable or biodegradable.

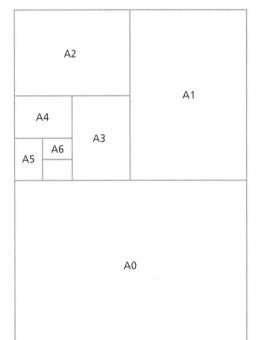

Paper sizes

Wood is cut, de-barked and turned into pulp   Wood pulp   Chemicals added (chalk and dye)   Mesh   Roll of paper

Manufacturing process for paper

Quick Test

1. Which type of card is excellent for printing on?
2. What does gsm stand for?
3. Why can't recycled paper be used for carton board?

Timber

You must be able to:

- Explain the difference between hardwood and softwood
- Describe the characteristics and common uses of a variety of woods and manufactured boards
- Explain how timber is converted into usable material.

Natural Timber

- Timber is the general name for wood materials.
- Properties can vary according to the direction of the grain.
- At the end of its usable life, wood can be burnt as fuel or broken down into fibres for use in manufactured boards. If put into landfill, wood is biodegradable.

Hardwood

- **Hardwoods** come from deciduous trees. They shed their leaves each autumn.

Hardwood	Characteristics	Typical Use
Oak	Very strong and hard, but easy to work with Open grained, light brown colour	High-quality furniture
Birch	Hard, but easy to work with Close, fine grain Pale, very light brown colour	Furniture and cabinets Turned items
Teak	Durable, oily wood that is resistant to moisture Golden brown colour	Outdoor furniture Marine/boat fittings
Balsa	Soft, can be marked using a finger Off-white to tan colour	Modelling

Deciduous tree (oak)

Softwood

- **Softwoods** come from coniferous trees.
- They maintain their foliage all year round, which is one reason why they typically grow faster than hardwood trees.
- Softwood from managed forests is a renewable resource: new trees are planted as each one is cut down.

Coniferous tree (pine)

Softwood	Characteristics	Typical Use
Pine	Fairly strong and durable, but easy to work with Straight grained Light brown or yellowish colour	Construction work and joinery, furniture
Cedar	Lightweight, can be up to 80% strength of oak, but relatively brittle Straight, uniform grain Pale reddish-brown colour	Lining drawers and chests Fencing
Spruce	Strong and hard, but low resistance to decay Straight grained Yellowish-white colour	General construction Wooden aircraft frames

Standard Sizes and Forms

- The tree trunks are cut into planks in a sawmill. Plank sizes are limited by the sizes of the tree trunks available.
- Planks are commonly available as rough sawn or planed square edge (PSE). PSE sizes are slightly smaller than rough sawn, as it has been planed to make it smooth.
- Wood is also available in a variety of standard sections called mouldings.

Manufactured Boards

- Manufactured boards are made by gluing wood fibres or veneers together.
- The fibres can be waste materials from the cutting of natural timber.
- The properties are typically uniform as there is no grain.
- The top layer of most manufactured boards can be a veneer from a high-quality wood to give a good appearance, or a plastic laminate for protection.
- Made in very large sheets of consistent quality; it is not limited by the size of the trees. The most common sheet size is 2440 × 1220 mm (8 × 4 ft).
- Sheets are available in standard thicknesses; for example, 3, 6, 9, 12 mm, etc.

Manufactured Board	Description	Typical Use	Appearance
Medium-density fibreboard (MDF)	Made from fine particles of timber, mixed with a bonding agent or glue and compressed Smooth, even surface, easily machined	Furniture, interior panelling	MDF
Plywood	Constructed from layers of veneer or plies which are glued together with the grain structure at 90° to each other Interior and exterior grades available	Furniture making Marine plywood is used for boat building	Plywood
Blockboard	Similar to plywood, but with central strips of timber	Shelving and worktops	Blockboard

Revise

Key Point

'Hardwood' and 'softwood' refers to the type of tree that the timber comes from, not the properties of the wood.

Trees in a forest after felling

Wood mouldings

Key Point

Manufactured boards offer consistent properties and more of the tree is used than for wood.

Key Words

grain
hardwood
softwood
veneer

Quick Test

1. Name three types of hardwood.
2. What does PSE stand for?
3. Name three types of manufactured board.

Metals

You must be able to:

- Explain the difference between ferrous and non-ferrous metals
- Describe the characteristics and common uses of a variety of metals
- Explain how metal ore is converted into usable material.

Making Metal

- Metal ore is mined or quarried from the ground.
- The metal is extracted from the ore by large-scale industrial processes requiring a massive amount of energy. The processes may involve heat, chemical reactions to remove unwanted elements or electrolysis.
- After extraction, metals are typically melted and either cast into products or shaped into stock forms.
- At the end of their usable life, metals can be recycled by melting them down and reprocessing into new products. This reduces the need to obtain new metal ore.

Opencast quarrying of iron ore

Ferrous Metals

- Ferrous metals contain iron.
- They are the most commonly used metals, with a huge variety of applications.
- Typically they have a melting point of 1600 °C or higher and most are silver-grey in colour.
- Most ferrous materials are prone to rusting and corrosion and can be picked up with a magnet (except stainless steel).

Smelting of metal

Ferrous Metal		Characteristics	Typical Use
Cast iron		Good hardness and compressive strength, but poor tensile strength and brittle under tension	Engine blocks, cookware, piping
Mild steel (low-carbon steel)		Tough, relatively low cost and easy to machine Prone to corrosion	Car body panels, nuts and bolts, engine parts
Stainless steel		An alloy of steel containing chromium Tough, strong and hard Difficult to machine Corrosion resistant	Kitchen equipment, medical instruments

Non-ferrous Metals

- Non-ferrous metals do not contain iron.
- They typically have good corrosion resistance, although they do tarnish.

- Non-ferrous materials are non-magnetic, so when sorting for recycling can be separated from ferrous materials using magnets.

Non-ferrous Metal		Characteristics	Typical Use
Aluminium		Lighter than steel, but not as strong	Drinks cans, cooking pans, food packaging
Copper		Excellent conductor of heat and electricity	Electrical wiring, water pipes
Tin		Relatively soft and malleable. Excellent corrosion resistance to water: used to plate steel containers to make 'tins' for food	Coating steel cans for corrosion resistance, alloying element in solder

Common Alloys

- Most metals are used as alloys.
- An alloy is a mixture of two or more metals, which has better properties than the pure metal.
- Alloys are created by melting the metals and adding them together.

Alloy	Main Constituents	Characteristics	Typical Use
Brass	Copper and zinc	Low friction, corrosion resistant, malleable	Locks, bearings, musical instruments
Pewter	Tin, copper and antimony	Low melting point (170–230 °C), easy to cast	Jewellery, decorative items
Solder	Tin and lead	Good electrical conductivity, low melting point (180–230 °C), reasonable strength	Attaching electrical components to circuit boards

Stock Forms

- Metals are available in a wide variety of standard shapes and sizes, including sheet, plate, round bar, square bar, square tube and round tube.
- As it requires much energy and effort to reform metal, designers normally try to either use a standard shape and size, or to use the closest size that requires the smallest amount of machining.
- Metal ingots can also be melted down and cast into complex shapes.

A variety of metal forms

Key Words

ferrous metal
alloy
non-ferrous metal
malleable

Quick Test

1. What is the meaning of the term 'alloy'?
2. Name three metal alloys.
3. Name four stock forms in which metal is available.

Polymers

You must be able to:

- Explain how polymers are converted into usable material
- Explain the difference between thermoplastic polymers and thermosetting polymers
- Describe the characteristics, common uses and available forms of a variety of polymers.

Making Polymers

- **Polymers** are made from chains of similar small chemical units, called monomers. The process of attaching the monomers together is called polymerisation.
- Most commonly used polymers are **synthetic**. They are manufactured from carbon-based **fossil fuels** using industrial-scale chemical processes.
- Fossil fuels are a **finite resource**. Extracting and transporting them has an impact on the environment.
- Synthetic polymers are not normally biodegradable.
- Polymers made from vegetable products are being developed. For example, corn starch polymer is already being used for food packaging. This is a **sustainable** polymer made from potatoes, corn and maize, and it is biodegradable.

Thermosetting Polymers

- **Thermosetting polymers** cannot soften when heated, but may char. Their polymer chains are interlinked with permanent chemical bonds.
- They are commonly available in liquid form (as resins) or as powders. They must be cured (heated) or reacted with chemicals to create the polymer.
- At the end of their usable life, thermosetting polymers typically end up being disposed of in landfill.

Key Point

Synthetic polymers are typically made from fossil fuels, a non-renewable resource.

Drilling for oil and gas out at sea

Key Point

Thermoplastics can be reshaped and recycled. Thermosetting polymers can not.

Thermosetting Polymer	Characteristics	Typical Use
Silicone	Non-reactive, resistant to extreme environments Silicone rubber is flexible but retains its shape well	Medical implants, non-stick coatings, sealants, lubricants
Epoxy resin	Made by mixing a chemical resin with a hardener Hard but brittle unless reinforced; resists chemicals well	Printed circuit boards, epoxy adhesive
Polyester resin	Made by mixing a chemical resin with a hardener Often reinforced with glass fibre to form the composite GRP Stiff, hard, but brittle unless laminated	Car bodies, boats
Urea formaldehyde	Hard, strong, stiff, excellent insulator but brittle	Plug sockets, electrical switches, door handles
Melamine formaldehyde	Heat resistant, hard, resists some chemicals and stains	Laminates for kitchen worktops

Thermoplastic Polymers

- **Thermoplastics** soften when they are heated and can be shaped when hot. When cooled they harden in the new shape, but can be reshaped again if reheated.
- Most thermoplastics are available in sheets of standard thickness, for example 1.5, 2 mm, etc. Some are also available as rods and blocks, as pellets or granules for injection moulding and as powders for dip-coating.
- Thermoplastic products are commonly marked to identify from which type of polymer they are made.
- If sorted into their different types, thermoplastics can be recycled.

Plastic granules used for injection moulding

Thermoplastic Polymer		Characteristics	Typical Use
PET	Polyethylene terephthalate	Transparent, commonly used for vacuum forming or blow moulding Softens at about 80 °C	Drinks bottles, food packaging
HDPE	High-density polyethylene	Strong, stiff Softens at about 130 °C	Pipes, bowls, buckets
LDPE	Low-density polyethylene	Flexible, soft, tough Softens at about 80–90 °C	Plastic bags, plastic film, squeezy toys
PVC	Polyvinylchloride	Stiff, hard wearing Softens at about 100–125 °C	Pipes, packaging, chemical tanks
PS	Polystyrene	An expanded polymer foam Low density, soft and spongy	Packaging, ceiling tiles
HIPS	High-impact polystyrene	Light, strong Softens at about 90 °C Commonly used in schools for vacuum forming	Packaging
PP	Polypropylene	Low density, tough and flexible Softens at about 140–150 °C	Ropes, carpets, packaging
ABS	Acrylonitrile butadiene styrene	Tough, impact resistant Softens at about 100 °C	Toys, protective headgear, canoes
PMMA	Polymethyl-methacrylate	Known by the trade names Acrylic and Perspex Hard wearing, can be transparent or coloured Softens between 85 and 165 °C depending on grade	Display signs, plastic windows, baths
TPE	Thermoplastic elastomers	A blend of polymers that possesses rubber-like behaviour, with good elasticity	Handles for power tools, plugs

Plastic recycling symbols showing the types of thermoplastic polymer

Key Words

polymer
synthetic
fossil fuel
finite resource
sustainable

thermosetting polymer
adhesive
thermoplastic

Quick Test

1. What are synthetic polymers commonly made from?
2. In which forms are thermosetting polymers typically available?
3. Name three typical uses of polypropylene.

Textiles

You must be able to:

- Describe the characteristics and common uses of a variety of textiles
- Explain how fabric is constructed from fibres
- Describe how the manufacture of textile products affects the environment.

Fibres and Fabrics

- Textiles is a general term used to describe any product that is made from a fabric.
- Fabric is made from fibres. These fine, hair-like particles range from short lengths (staple fibres) to continuous filaments.
- Individual fibres are weak, so they are spun and twisted together to produce yarn.

Fabric Construction

- **Knitted** fabrics are made from yarns in a series of interlocking loops. Loops may be arranged in different ways, called weft and warp.
- Knitted fabrics are warm and stretchy (elastic).
- **Woven** fabrics are constructed from interlocking yarns or threads. There are several different types of weave.
- The fabric has a grain due to the direction of the threads. It is strongest along the straight grain of the fabric when the weave is close and firm, but lacks elasticity.
- Woven fabric has a **selvedge** – an edge that will not fray. However, the fabric will fray easily when cut.
- Non-woven fabrics (such as felt) are made from raw fibres, rather than yarns.
- They may be made by using chemicals to mat the fibres together, using heat to bond the fibres or stitching the fibres in layers and interlocking them.

Natural Fibres

- **Natural fibres** come from animals or plants.
- Animal fibres include wool, silk, alpaca, angora, camel hair, cashmere, mohair and vicuña.
- Plant fibres include cotton, linen, jute, hemp and ramie.
- Natural fibres are biodegradable.

Key Point

Fabrics are constructed from fibres by knitting, weaving or non-woven methods.

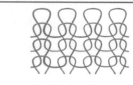

Weft-knitted fabric

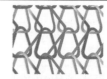

Warp-knitted fabric

Non-woven fabric

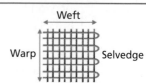

Weft / Warp / Selvedge

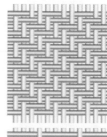

Fabric construction

Natural Fibre	Sources and Characteristics	Typical Uses
Cotton	A vegetable/cellulose fibre, from the ripened seeds of the cotton plant. Strong, durable, absorbent, creases easily	Denim, calico, flannelette, gabardine. Underwear, shirts and blouses, T-shirts, jeans
Wool	An animal/protein fibre, from the fleeces of sheep. Warm, soft, absorbent, crease resistant	Felt, flannel, gabardine. Jumpers, suits, dresses, carpets

Natural Fibre	Sources and Characteristics	Typical Uses
Silk	An animal/protein fibre, from the cocoon of the silk moth Smooth, lustrous and strong	Chiffon, organza, crepe, velvet Dresses, shirts, ties

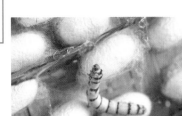

Group of cocoons and a silkworm

Synthetic Fibres

- **Synthetic fibres** are human-made, typically from oil.
- Oil is a fossil fuel. It is a finite resource, so once it is used it is not naturally replaced quickly. Extracting and transporting oil can cause environmental damage or pollution.
- The oil is processed using large-scale industrial processes to extract the chemicals needed to make the fibres.
- Synthetic fibres are not typically biodegradable.

Synthetic Fibre	Characteristics	Typical Use
Polyamide (Nylon)	Produced from two different chemical monomers Strong, durable, warm, crease resistant	Tights and stockings, sportswear, upholstery, carpets
Polyester	Produced from oil Strong, durable, elastic, crease resistant	Sportswear
Acrylic	Produced from oil Soft and warm, similar to wool	Clothing, fake fur, furnishings

Blended Fibres

- Blended fibres use a mixture of different types of fibre. They combine the properties of different fibres.
- One of the best known is polycotton. This is used for 'quick-drying' towels, as it combines the absorbency of cotton with the quick-drying properties of polyester.

Denim jeans

Textile Processing and the Environment

- When cutting textile products from fabric, consideration should be given to the layout of the pattern to minimise waste material.
- In addition to the chemicals and energy required to make the fibres and fabrics, most textile products are dyed and finished. These processes use lots of chemicals, such as dyes, resins to make fabrics shrink-proof or softeners to improve the feel of the fabric.
- Textile products can often be reused; for example, they can be sold on through a charity shop or recycled, with the materials used to make another product.
- At the end of their usable life, most textile products are incinerated or go to landfill.

Polycotton towels

Dying cloth by hand

Quick Test

1. Name three different types of fabric construction.
2. Name three natural fibres.
3. What is acrylic made from?

Key Words

yarn   selvedge   synthetic
knitted   natural   fibres
woven   fibres

New Developments in Materials

You must be able to:

- Describe the characteristics and uses of a variety of new materials
- Explain what is meant by a composite material.

Biopolymers

- **Biopolymers** are polymers produced by living organisms.
- They are used to make disposable cutlery, packaging such as food trays and thin films for wrapping.
- Polyethylene (which is normally made from the fossil fuel oil) can be made from biomass by a fermentation process.
- Biopolymers such as polylactic acid (PLA), zein and poly-3-hydroxybutyrate can be used as replacements for polystyrene- or polyethylene-based synthetic polymers.
- They are biodegradable, carbon-neutral, renewable and suitable to be composted.

Nanomaterials

- **Nanomaterials** are made up of particles that are less than 100 nm (nanometres) in size.
- They are small enough to enter the bloodstream and deliver drugs around the body.
- Nanomaterial coatings for glass and fabrics can repel dirt or water, giving 'self-cleaning' properties.
- There are concerns that we do not understand how the increased use of nanomaterials will affect the environment or human health.

Graphene

- **Graphene** is a form of carbon. Its atoms are arranged hexagonally in a flat 2D layer, just one atom thick.
- It is about 200 times stronger than steel, flexible, transparent and conducts heat and electricity well.
- Potential applications include solar cells, touch panels and smart windows for phones.
- The high cost to manufacture graphene has limited its use to date, but new manufacturing processes are being developed which make it at much lower cost.

Superalloys

- **Superalloys** are metal alloys with excellent strength, corrosion resistance and resistance to creep (a type of failure that can occur at high temperatures).

Key Point

New materials with improved properties are constantly being developed.

Biopolymer knife and fork

Structure of graphene

Potential graphene application: a flexible screen

Inside view of an aircraft jet engine

- Over 50% by weight of the parts used in advanced aircraft engines, such as turbine blades, are made from superalloys.

Technical Textiles

- Technical textiles are manufactured for performance properties rather than visual appearance.
- This includes fabrics designed to provide protection from injury or hazardous environments; for example:
  - Kevlar in body armour provides protection from weapon impact
  - Marlan, used for protective clothing in foundries, provides protection from heat and metal splashes.
- Conductive fibres allow circuits to be incorporated into fabrics. These may be weaved or knitted into another fabric, or applied by printing or layering. These can be used to make temperature-controlled clothing or to integrate lights into emergency clothing.
- Power-assisted textiles incorporate a power source that can power other products, such as a mobile phone. Power sources may include solar panels, flexible batteries or devices to turn the kinetic energy of human movement into electricity.
- Textiles can also incorporate electronic systems, such as MP3 players, GPS systems and sensors to monitor body temperature or pulse rate. They can even send the data to medical professionals so that the wearer can be monitored remotely.

Policeperson in body armour

Composites

- Composites combine the properties of two or more materials.
- Weight for weight, a carbon fibre reinforced composite can have up to six times the strength of steel.
- Unlike an alloy, the materials in a composite are not mixed at a chemical level: if you look at the material under a microscope you can see the separate materials in contact with each other.
- Common composites include:
  - glass-reinforced polyester (GRP) and fibreglass, used in car body building and repair and in boat hulls
  - carbon-reinforced polyester (CRP) used to make tent poles, high-performance bicycles and sports equipment
  - reinforced concrete, used to make large buildings.
- As the materials are not easily separated, composites cannot normally be recycled. At the end of their usable life they are normally disposed of to landfill.

Sir Bradley Wiggins in the Tour de France riding a bicycle made from composite materials

Quick Test

1. Which chemical element is graphene comprised of?
2. What size are the particles in nanomaterials?
3. Name three composite materials.

Key Words

biopolymer
nanomaterial
graphene
superalloy
technical textile
composite

Standard Components

You must be able to:

- Explain why standard components are used
- List standard components used with a variety of different materials.

Reasons for using Standard Components

- Some types of component are used in many different products.
- They include fasteners and fixings to hold materials together, electrical components and mechanical parts.
- To make these parts in small quantities can be very expensive, due to the time and equipment required. For example, making one staple to attach some sheets of paper together would require a piece of material to be bought, the tools to cut it and bend it, and the time to make it.
- There are companies that have production lines dedicated to just making these standard components. This means they can:
  - buy materials in bulk, getting lower prices
  - divide the equipment cost across millions of parts
  - automate the processes and use labour efficiently
  - ensure that the consistency and quality of the products is maintained.
- The standard parts can then be bought at low cost by whoever needs them. The parts are normally available in a range of standard sizes. Designers normally take this into consideration when designing new products.

Key Point

Standard components are parts that are used in many different products.

Key Point

It is much cheaper to buy a standard component than to make a small quantity of the part.

Types of Standard Component

• Used with paper and boards:
  – clips
  – fasteners, for example plastic rivets, sticky tape
  – bindings.
	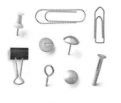
	Paper fasteners

		Plastic binder
			
			Two parts of the clic rivet
			The base of the slit is straight
			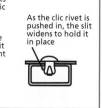
			As the clic rivet is pushed in, the slit widens to hold it in place
			Plastic rivets

• Used with timber:
  – hinges
  – brackets
  – screws
  – nails
  – handles, drawer runners and knock-down fittings.

	Door hinge
		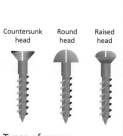
		Countersunk head Round head Raised head
		Types of screw
			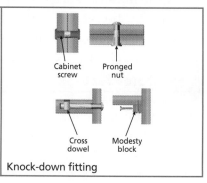
			Cabinet screw Pronged nut Cross dowel Modesty block
			Knock-down fitting

- Used with polymers:
  - caps
  - fasteners
  - nuts, bolts and washers.

Plastic nuts and bolts

Plastic caps

- Used with fibres and fabrics:
  - zips
  - buttons
  - poppers and press studs
  - Velcro
  - decorative items, such as embroidered decals, sequins and beads.

Zips

Buttons

Press stud

Velcro

- Used with metals:
  - nuts, bolts and washers
  - rivets
  - hinges.

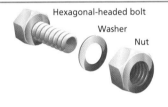

Bolt, washer and nut

Countersunk   Cheese   Domed

Raised   Round   Socket

Screws

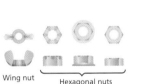

Rivet heads

Rivets

Wing nut   Hexagonal nuts

Nuts and bolts

Washers

- Electrical components used in control systems and circuits:
  - resistors
  - capacitors
  - diodes, including LEDs
  - transistors and drivers
  - microcontrollers
  - switches
  - motors.

Resistors

Microcontroller

Capacitors

Diodes

LEDs

- Mechanical components:
  - levers
  - linkages
  - gears
  - cams
  - pulleys
  - belts.

Metal gears

Plastic gears

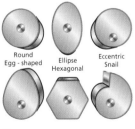

Round Egg-shaped   Ellipse Hexagonal   Eccentric Snail

Cams

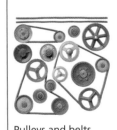

Pulleys and belts

Quick Test

1. Name a type of standard component that is used with both metal and wood.
2. Name six standard mechanical components.

Key Words

standard components

Review Questions

Communicating Design Ideas

1 Explain **one** application of **each** of the following graphical techniques in design and technology.

a) 2D or 3D sketches

....

....

....

....

b) Exploded drawings

....

....

....

....

c) Flow charts

....

....

....

.... [6]

2 Discuss the importance of collaboration across material areas when designing solutions to problems. Use examples to support your answer.

[12]

Practice Questions

Material Considerations

1. Name the material property described by each of the following statements.

   a) The ability of a material to resist wear or being scratched

   .... [1]

   b) The ability of heat to pass through a material

   .... [1]

   c) How easily a material burns

   .... [1]

2. a) Give **two** examples of how social considerations may influence the choice of materials for a product.

   ....

   ....

   ....

   .... [2]

   b) Explain why the availability of stock forms of material may influence the design and choice of which material to use for a product.

   ....

   ....

   ....

   ....

   ....

   ....

   ....

   .... [4]

3 Complete the table below, filling in the characteristics and typical uses of different types of paper and board. The first line has been completed as an example.

Type	Characteristics	Typical Use
Cartridge paper	Tough and lightly textured Typically a light cream colour	Drawing
Layout and tracing paper	[2]	[1]
Bleached card	[2]	[1]
Corrugated cardboard	[2]	[1]
Foil-lined board	[2]	[1]
Polypropylene sheet	[2]	[1]

Practice Questions

4 **a)** **i)** Name a softwood.

_____ [1]

ii) Give a typical use for this softwood.

_____ [1]

iii) Explain why this softwood is an appropriate choice for this application.

_____

_____ [2]

b) **i)** Name a hardwood.

_____ [1]

ii) Give a typical use for this hardwood.

_____ [1]

iii) Explain why this hardwood is an appropriate choice for this application.

_____

_____ [2]

5 Name **two** stock forms in which timber is available.

1. _____ [1]

2. _____ [1]

6 Using notes and/or sketches, describe the processes involved in converting metals from their raw materials to finished products.

[4]

7 Complete the table, filling in the missing information about metals. The first line has been completed as an example.

Type	Name	Characteristics	Typical Use
Ferrous	Mild steel	Tough, prone to corrosion	Car body panels
a)	Aluminium	Not as strong as steel but lighter	b)
Ferrous alloy	c)	Tough, strong and hard Corrosion resistant	Medical instruments
Non-ferrous	d)	Excellent conductor	Electrical wiring
Non-ferrous alloy	Brass	e)	f)

[6]

Practice Questions

8 Complete the table, naming **one** thermosetting polymer and **two** thermoplastic polymers. For each, give a typical application.

	Name	Typical Application
Thermosetting polymer	a)	b)
Thermoplastic polymer	c)	d)
Thermoplastic polymer	e)	f)

[6]

9 Explain the difference between a thermoplastic and a thermosetting polymer.

....

....

....

....

....

....

[4]

10 Using notes and/or sketches, explain the differences between knitted and woven fabrics.

[4]

11 a) Describe the structure and properties of graphene.

[4]

b) State **three** potential applications of graphene.

1.

2.

3. [3]

12 Name **two** parts used in electrical circuits that are commonly available as standard components.

1.

2. [2]

Total Marks _____ / 67

Finishing Materials

You must be able to:

- Explain the purpose of finishing materials
- Describe how finishing techniques are applied to a range of materials.

Purpose of Finishing

- The main reasons for finishing materials are to improve function or aesthetics.
- Functional considerations include durability and added resistance to overcome environmental factors. For example, painting wood to be used on an outdoor fence helps to make it water resistant.
- Some materials are self-finishing and so do not need a specialist finish to be applied.

Finishing Metals

- Polishing:
  - Polishing relies on cutting the surface of the metal until it is very smooth. Abrasive liquids can be applied to aid in this process.
  - Waxes or non-abrasive liquids can be used to fill in any subsequent gaps in the metal.
- Coating:
  - Dip-coating involves blowing air through the powder to make it behave like a liquid, dipping the metal in the fluid and heating it to form a smooth finish.
  - Powder coating is a more sophisticated version of dip-coating where the powder is sprayed onto the metal. Powder and object are electrically charged to attract an even coat and then heated.
- Anodising:
  - Anodising provides a corrosion-resistant finish to aluminium.
  - It involves electrolysis and the addition of colour.
- Plating:
  - Plating uses electrolysis to create a thin, corrosion-resistant layer of protection.
  - Chrome plating is the most widely used method of plating.
- Galvanising:
  - Metal, often mild steel, is dipped into a bath of molten zinc.

Metals being powder coated in an industrial environment

Finishing Plastics

- The main finishing technique for plastics is polishing.
  - Hard plastics such as acrylic are often polished on their cut edges.
  - Polishing also removes fine scratches.

- Polish can be applied by hand using a cloth, or by applying a compound with a buffing wheel.
- Many plastics are self-finishing.

Finishing Timber-Based Materials

- Sanding sealer:
  - This is a solvent-based finish that is used to seal timber.
  - It is used as a first coat before applying varnish or wax polish.
- Varnishing:
  - Polyurethane varnish is a tough, heat-proof and waterproof finish available in different colours.
  - It is usually applied in three coats with a brush. It can then be smoothed with fine glasspaper.
- Wax polish:
  - Wax fills the porous surface of the timber, building up a layer of polish on the surface of the material.
  - It can be applied by hand, with a cloth or via a buffing wheel.

Varnish being applied to a piece of wood

Finishing Fabrics

- Water-repelling finishes:
  - A silicon-based chemical is sprayed onto the fabric.
  - This provides a water-repellent layer.
- Flame-proofing:
  - Chemicals are applied to fabrics such as cotton and linen.
  - This provides a protective layer that slows down the burning process.
- Bleaching:
  - Bleaching removes all natural colour from the fabric.
  - It is applied to cotton and linen, which it can weaken.

Finishing Paper-Based Materials

- Laminating:
  - In laminating, plastic film is applied on one or both sides of paper or card.
  - This adds rigidity and a waterproof layer of protection that can be easily wiped clean.
- Embossing:
  - Steel dies are used to press a shape onto the material.
  - This gives a tactile effect and improves the visual look of the product.
- Foil applications:
  - A design is stamped onto the material through metal foil.
  - This is used to enhance the look of the material.

Many outdoor coats are finished to make them water repellent

 Key Point

Laminating paper or card adds a waterproof layer of protection that can be wiped clean.

 Key Words

self-finishing material
polishing
varnishing
bleaching
laminating

Quick Test

1. What are the main reasons for finishing materials?
2. What is a self-finishing material?
3. What is the main way of finishing plastics?

Structural Integrity

You must be able to:

- Explain why reinforcement is used in structures
- Describe different types of reinforcement used in structures.

Structures and Reinforcement

- A structure is an object that is constructed from parts. Examples of structures include the Eiffel Tower, bicycle frames, school blazers and chairs.
- Often, structures need to be reinforced or stiffened so that they can achieve the properties that are needed from them.
- Using reinforcement means that a structure can be made at a lower cost or with less weight than making the whole thing from one solid piece of material, but that it is still strong and rigid enough to fulfil its purpose.
- There are many different ways to reinforce structures. The type of reinforcement used will depend upon:
  - the type of product being reinforced
  - the material that it is made from
  - the properties that are needed.

> **Key Point**
>
> Structures are reinforced to achieve or improve their properties.

Buildings and Bridges

- Large structures, such as bridges, are often reinforced by triangulation. Triangulation uses structural members to form triangles to increase the strength.

Triangles in a bridge structure

- When concrete is used to make buildings, this is normally reinforced using steel bars. This creates a composite material.

Concrete being poured over steel reinforcement bars

Textile Products

- **Boning** is where rigid strips of material are used to hold the shape of a textile item, such as a bodice. These strips of material are known as bones or stays. Originally, they were often made from whalebone. Most modern strips are made from plastic, but steel wires are used in some products.
- **Darts** are a type of fold or tuck in the fabric of a garment. They are sewn into the fabric and come to a point, providing shape. They are often used to help the garment fit to the shape of the person wearing it, for example around the bust, waist or hips.
- **Layering** involves adding extra materials to a textile product to increase its strength or to make it more rigid. Interfacing is a type of layering that is often used in shirt collars to make them stiff. It is used on the unseen or 'wrong' side of the fabric, for instance where buttonholes will be sewn.

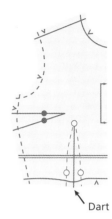

Dart

Boxes and Casings

- Boxes and casings are often made from sheets of plastic or metal. Reinforcement is used to ensure that they are strong and do not bend easily.
- Ribs are used to increase the rigidity of a sheet of material. They are long raised pieces of material. Ribs can be formed by adding extra material or by pressing or moulding the shape into the surface.
- Ribs on the inside of a plastic casing are called webbing.

> **Key Point**
>
> There are many different ways of reinforcing structures.

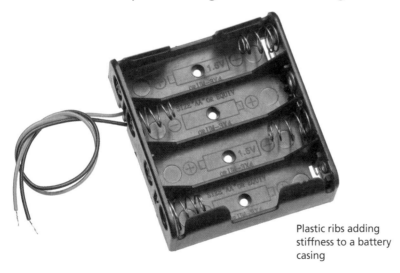

Plastic ribs adding stiffness to a battery casing

> **Quick Test**
>
> 1. State three reasons why reinforcement might be used in a structure.
> 2. What shape is most often used to reinforce large structures?
> 3. Name two types of reinforcement that help clothes maintain their shape.

> **Key Words**
>
> reinforcing
> triangulation
> boning
> darts
> layering

Motion and Levers

You must be able to:

- Describe the four types of motion
- Describe the basic principles of a lever
- Explain the different classes of lever.

Types of Motion

- Most products and systems involve some form of motion.
- There are four types of motion:
  - **Rotating** motion means movement in a circle.
  - **Linear** motion goes straight in one direction.
  - **Reciprocating** motion means moving backwards and forwards.
  - **Oscillating** motion means swinging backwards and forwards, like a pendulum.

Principles of Levers

- **Levers** are a simple form of machine. They change the amount of **effort** or force needed to move a load.
- They consist of a rigid bar or beam that pivots around a fixed point called a **fulcrum**.
- A load is applied at one position on the lever.
- Effort is applied at another position on the lever. Sufficient effort results in movement of the lever about the fulcrum.
- Changing the distances between the fulcrum and either the load or the effort changes the amount of effort needed to move the load.
- There are three classes (or types) of lever: first, second and third class.

First-Class Lever

- In a first-class lever, the fulcrum is between the load and the effort.
- If the effort is further from the fulcrum than the load is, this results in a mechanical advantage. This means that the effort needed to move the lever is less than the load.
- The amount of mechanical advantage is proportional to the distance of the effort from the fulcrum and the distance of the load from the fulcrum.

Rotating

Linear

Reciprocating

Oscillating

Types of motion

Key Point

There are four types of motion: rotating, linear, reciprocating and oscillating.

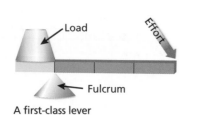

A first-class lever

- The distance that the effort and the load move is also proportional to the mechanical advantage.
- For example: if the effort is two times the distance from the fulcrum that the load is, the effort needed to move the load will be half of the value of the load. The distance that the effort will move will be double the distance that the load will move.
- Seesaws and scissors are examples of first-class levers.

Second-Class Lever

- In a second-class lever, the load is applied between the effort and the fulcrum.
- There is a mechanical advantage because the load is nearer the fulcrum than the effort.
- Nutcrackers and wheelbarrows are examples of second-class levers.

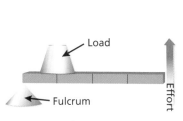 

A second-class lever

Third-Class Lever

- In a third-class lever, the effort is applied between the load and the fulcrum.
- The effort needed for movement is greater than the load, because the effort is nearer the fulcrum than the load. However, the amount of movement of the load is multiplied.
- Lifting a dumbbell is an example of a third-class lever: the load is the dumbbell, the fulcrum is the elbow and the effort is provided by the biceps muscle that attaches to the forearm between them.

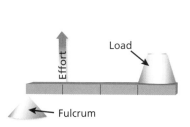 

A third-class lever

> **Quick Test**
>
> 1. What is the difference between reciprocating and oscillating motion?
> 2. What are the four common features of all levers?
> 3. Which type of lever does not give a mechanical advantage to the effort?

> **Key Words**
>
> rotating
> linear
> reciprocating
> oscillating
> lever
> effort
> fulcrum

Mechanical Devices

You must be able to:

- Describe how linkages, cams, gears and pulleys transfer motion
- Explain how these mechanical devices are used to change the magnitude and direction of forces.

Mechanical Devices

- Mechanical devices are used to transfer motion or force between mechanisms or to convert between different types of motion.

Linkages

- **Linkages** are used to transfer motion between two positions. However, they can also act as levers (for example, in scissors).
- A push–pull linkage can reverse the direction of linear motion. It is also called a reversing linkage.
- The input to a tongs linkage is an oscillating motion. This extends the tongs (linear motion) and provides an output of oscillating motion. These are used in extending arm 'grabbers'.
- A 'moving wings' linkage changes reciprocating motion to oscillating motion.

Push-pull   Tongs   Moving wings

Extends

Linkages

Cams

- **Cams** are typically used to convert rotary motion to reciprocating motion.
- A follower is a rod that is moved as the cam rotates. This is normally connected to the object that is to be moved.
- A follower can only rise (go up), dwell (be held at the same height) or fall (go down). How long it spends doing each of these depends on the shape of the cam.
- Cams come in many different shapes, including eccentric circles, pear-shaped and snail-shaped. The different shapes give different amounts of time spent rising, dwelling or falling.

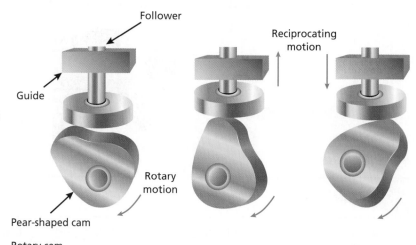

Follower

Reciprocating motion

Guide

Rotary motion

Pear-shaped cam

Rotary cam

- A guide might be used to keep the follower in the correct place.
- Cams are used to provide the reciprocating movement of the needle in a sewing machine.

Gears

- **Gears** have teeth that mesh with the teeth of other gears. Gears that work together must have teeth of the same size.
- Gears can change the speed or force of the motion they transfer. This is in proportion to the number of teeth they have. If a small gear turns a big gear with twice as many teeth, the big gear will rotate at half the speed of the small gear – but with twice the force.
- Spur gears transfer rotary motion. When using just two gears, the direction of movement is reversed. These are the most common gear used in gearboxes.
- Bevel gears change rotary motion through 90°. These are used in hand drills.
- A worm and worm wheel also change rotary motion through 90°. The worm gear is the driver (input) and has a single spiral tooth. This means that worm and worm wheels give a very large reduction in speed and a high torque (twisting force).
- A rack and pinion can be used to change rotary motion into linear motion. These are used in car steering or to move the base on a pillar drill up or down.

Spur gears

Bevel gear

Worm and worm wheel

Rack and pinion

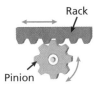

Types of gear

Pulleys

- A **pulley** is a pair of grooved wheels with a belt running in the groove.
- This transfers rotary motion, with both wheels moving in the same direction. If the belt is crossed over, the two wheels will run in opposite directions.
- Like gears, pulleys can change the speed or force of the motion they transfer. This is in proportion to the radius of the pulley.
- The belt can move or stretch to adsorb shocks. However, if it is too loose or the force being transmitted is too high, the belt will slip and some (or even all) of the motion will not be transferred. Toothed belts can be used to reduce the risk of slippage, but they are not able to transmit the same amount of force as gears.
- Pulleys are often used in machines to transmit force from the motor to the tool – for example drills, lathes and sewing machines.

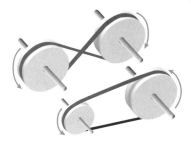

Pulleys

> **Key Point**
>
> In gears and pulleys, the speed and force transferred is proportional to the sizes of the two parts.

> **Key Words**
>
> linkage
> cam
> gear
> pulley

> **Quick Test**
>
> 1. Cams are used to change between which types of motion?
> 2. Name four types of gear.
> 3. What would be the effect of crossing over the belt in a pulley?

Electronic Systems

You must be able to:

- Describe the main stages that make up an electronic system
- Select appropriate input, process and output devices for use in products.

Structure of a System

- **Electronic systems** are made up of input, process and output stages. Some also include a driver stage.
- **Input devices** take a 'real-world' signal, such as light, sound or movement, and turn it into an electronic signal, such as a voltage or current. Common examples are switches and sensors.
- **Processes** act like the 'brain' of a system. They alter the electronic signal to create functions such as timing and counting.
- Drivers increase the signal going into the output stage of the system. This ensures that output devices can draw the required amount of current to work effectively.
- **Output devices** take an electronic signal and turn it into a real-world signal. For example, speakers produce sound and light-emitting diodes (LEDs) produce light.

> **Key Point**
>
> Electronic systems consist of input, process and output stages, with drivers added as appropriate.

Systems Block Diagrams

- Electronic systems can be represented as block diagrams.
- Block diagrams present a 'top-down' overview of the system and how it will work.
- The arrows represent the signals going into and out of each block.
- The blocks represent the components or groups of components that alter the signals.

A young child using a night light

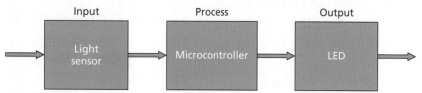

A block diagram for a child's night light

- In the example a light sensor, such as a light-dependent resistor (LDR), would detect the light level of the child's bedroom. The microcontroller could be used to turn the LED on for a timed period when it gets dark.

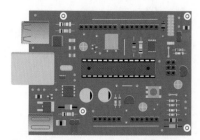

An electronic system assembled on a printed circuit board (PCB)

Electronic System Components

- Some of the main components used in electronic systems are shown in the table.

Component Name	Circuit Symbol	Input, Process or Output	What it Does
Push to make switch		Input	Allows current to flow through it when pressed
Tilt switch		Input	Allows current to flow through it when tilted
Light-dependent resistor		Input	Has a resistance that changes depending on the light level
Infrared sensor		Input	Detects infrared light coming from objects within its range
Light-emitting diode		Output	Produces light when current flows from the anode to the cathode
Buzzer		Output	Produces a buzzing sound when current flows through it
Speaker		Output	Turns electronic signals into sounds
Motor		Output	Produces rotary motion when current flows through it

A light-dependent resistor (LDR)

A light-emitting diode (LED)

A speaker

> ### Key Point
>
> Input devices respond to, and output devices produce, light, sound or movement.

Quick Test

1. What are the four main stages that often make up a complete electronic system?
2. How do light-dependent resistors work?
3. What output devices can be used to produce light, sound and movement?

> ### Key Words
>
> electronic system
> input device
> process
> output device

Programmable Components

You must be able to:

- Describe the main uses of programmable components in products
- Discuss the different programming methods that can be used.

What are Programmable Components?

- Programmable components are electronic components that can be programmed to perform different functions.
- They can replace more traditional process blocks in an electronic system, such as timers, counters and logic gates. They can be used to add intelligence to products, such as in robots or children's toys.
- One commonly used example of a programmable component is a microcontroller. This is a small computer on a single integrated circuit, or IC. Integrated circuits are found in products ranging from dishwashers to mobile phones to highly complex aircraft guidance systems.
- A microcontroller has ports for the connection of input and output devices, such as sensors, buzzers and LEDs (light-emitting diodes).
- When using output devices that draw a high current, such as motors, it is often necessary to add a suitable driver circuit. Two commonly used examples of these are Darlington pairs and MOSFETs.

A programmable IC

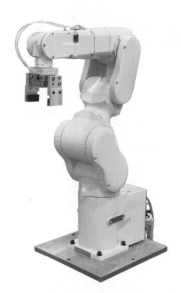

A programmable robot arm

Advantages and Disadvantages of Using Programmable Components

- Before deciding whether to use a programmable component in a product it is important to consider their advantages and disadvantages.

Advantages

- They can often be reprogrammed hundreds of thousands of times, making them very flexible.
- They can support a wide range of different input and output devices, whereas many traditional ICs are limited in this respect.
- One programmable component can often replace a number of traditional ICs in a system, thus reducing the size of circuits.

Disadvantages

- Access to suitable programming software and/or hardware is needed.
- Some programmable components can be expensive, although this cost is reducing over time.

Key Point

Programmable components allow designers to embed functionality and intelligence into products.

How Programmable Components are Programmed

- There are three main ways of programming a programmable component: flow chart software, block based editors and raw program code.
- Using flow chart software and block editors means that programmers do not need to have an in-depth knowledge of raw code. These are also very visual forms of programming, which are easy to read and understand. However, they can be limiting when complex programs are needed.
- Programming languages such as BASIC and C++ allow for more complex programming, but require more skill from the programmer.
- Almost all modern programmable components can now be programmed whilst 'in circuit'.

Flow Chart Programming Symbols

- Some of the main symbols used in flow chart programming are shown below.

Symbol	Name of Symbol	Example Use in a Program
(rounded rectangle)	Start/End	Clearly marking the start or end of a program.
(parallelogram)	Input/Output	Turning an LED or other output device 'on' or 'off'.
(rectangle)	Process	'Wait' command for pausing a program for a set time.
(diamond)	Decision	Checking to see whether a switch is 'on' or 'off'.
(subroutine symbol)	Subroutine	Creating a 'program within a program' that can be 'called' when needed.

Start

G1 On? N

Y

High GO

Wait 5s

Low GO

Stop

A simple flow chart timer program for a microcontroller. This program could be used to turn on an LED for 5 seconds when a switch is pressed.

> ### Key Point
>
> Programmable components must be programmed using suitable programming software and/or hardware.

Quick Test

1. What is a programmable component?
2. What are the advantages of using programmable components?
3. What are the three main methods of programming programmable components?

> ### Key Words
>
> microcontroller
> integrated circuit (IC)
> driver circuit

Review Questions

Material Considerations

1 State the meaning of the following properties.

   a) Tensile strength

   ....

   .... [1]

   b) Density

   ....

   .... [1]

   c) Durability

   ....

   .... [1]

2 A designer is designing a toy for babies. Discuss the aesthetic considerations the designer may
   make when selecting the material.

   ....

   ....

   ....

   ....

   ....

   ....

   ....

   ....

   ....

   .... [6]

3 Using notes and/or sketches, describe the processes involved in converting paper from its raw material to a finished product.

[6]

4 **a)** State **two** typical applications for foam board.

1. ....

2. .... [1]

b) Explain how the use of foam board affects the environment.

....

....

....

....

[4]

5 Explain the differences between hardwood and softwood.

[4]

6 Using notes and/or sketches, describe the processes involved in making plywood from its raw materials into a finished board.

[4]

7 **a)** State what is meant by the term 'alloy'.

.... [1]

b) **i)** Name a ferrous metal alloy.

.... [1]

ii) Give a typical use for this alloy.

.... [1]

iii) Explain why this alloy is an appropriate choice for this application.

....

....

....

.... [2]

c) **i)** Name a non-ferrous metal alloy.

.... [1]

ii) Give a typical use for this alloy.

....

.... [1]

iii) Explain why this alloy is an appropriate choice for this application.

....

....

....

.... [2]

Review Questions

8   Discuss how the increased use of polymers may affect the environment.

....

....

....

....

....

....

....

....

....

....

....

....

....

....

....

....

....   [10]

9 Explain the difference between natural and synthetic fibres.

_____

_____

_____ [2]

10 The pie chart below shows how the market for technical textiles in a country is divided into different sectors.

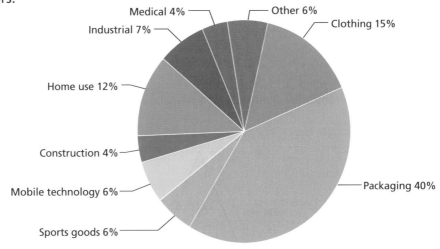

a) The total value of the market is £40 million.

Calculate the value of the segment for home use.

_____

_____

_____ [2]

b) Calculate the fraction of the total market value that is for clothing.

Give your answer as a fraction in its lowest form.

_____

_____ [1]

11 Name two mechanical parts that are commonly available as standard components.

1. _____

2. _____ [2]

Total Marks _____ / 54

Technical Understanding

1 A company is designing the structure for the frame of a racing bicycle. Explain why they would use a reinforced frame rather than one made from a solid piece of material.

....

....

....

.... [3]

2 The figure shows an isosceles triangle. It is part of the reinforcement structure in a crane.

Calculate the angle a.

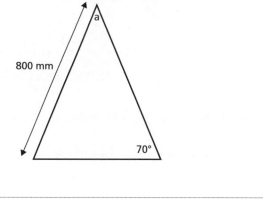

....

....

....

.... [2]

3 State what is meant by each of the following types of motion.

a) Linear

.... [1]

b) Rotating

.... [1]

c) Reciprocating

.... [1]

d) Oscillating

....

[1]

4 **a)** Give an example of a product that acts as a first-class lever.

....

[1]

b) A second-class lever is giving a mechanical advantage of 3.

Calculate the effort needed to move a load of 24 Newtons.

....

....

....

[2]

5 For each of the following, name a mechanical device which can be used to:

a) Reverse the direction of a linear movement

....

[1]

b) Transfer rotary movement through 90°

....

[1]

c) Convert rotary movement to reciprocating movement

....

[1]

d) Convert rotary movement into linear motion.

....

[1]

6 The diagram below shows a lever.

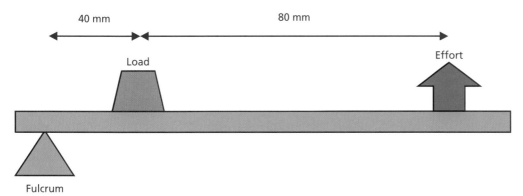

a) State the class of the lever.

.... [1]

b) The load is 40 mm from the fulcrum. The effort is 80 mm from the load.

📇 Calculate the mechanical advantage.

....

....

.... [2]

7 Two gears similar to those shown are being used to transfer motion in a mechanical device.

Gears (not to scale)

a) Name the type of gear shown.

.... [1]

b) The input (driver) gear is turning clockwise. What is the direction of the output (driven) gear?

.... [1]

c) Imagine that the input gear had 12 teeth and the output gear had 36 teeth.

📇 Calculate the gear ratio.

....

....

.... [2]

8 **a)** Name an electronic sensor that can be used to detect changes in light level.

_____ [1]

b) Name an output device that produces each of the following:

Light _____

Sound _____

Movement _____ [3]

c) Describe the function of a tilt switch.

_____

_____ [2]

9 **a)** Give one specific example of a programmable component.

_____ [1]

b) Explain **one** reason why designers use programmable components in products.

_____

_____ [2]

c) Explain **one** disadvantage of using programmable components in products.

_____

_____ [2]

Total Marks _____ / 35

Modelling Processes

You must be able to:

- Explain why designers produce models of their ideas
- Describe how tools, equipment and processes are used to create models of design ideas
- Discuss the use of different modelling materials for different applications.

Physical Models

- Designers make **models** of their ideas to check how they will look and function in 3D. They can also be presented to clients and stakeholders to gain feedback.
- Making models ensures that problems with the design are found early, before the design is manufactured using more expensive materials.
- Models are usually scaled down, but can be full size depending on the design or the stage in the design process.
- Modelling is a key part of the iterative design process. Each iteration of a model can be evaluated, tested and then refined.

Key Point

Modelling is a key part of the iterative design process.

Materials and Processes Used When Making Models

- Common materials for modelling are card, rigid foam, polystyrene blocks and cheap timber-based materials, such as thin MDF or balsa wood.
- Card:
  - Card is commonly used for making early or rough models of designs as it is cheap and easy to cut.
  - Card can be cut using scissors or craft knives. Safety rules and/or rotary trimmers can be used when straight lines are needed.
  - Pieces of card can be attached together using masking tape or hot glue guns.
- Polystyrene block:
  - This is very useful for making solid **concept models**.
  - It can be cut using saws or a hot-wire foam cutter.
  - Rectangular or square blocks can be sanded into more complex shapes.
  - Pieces can be joined together using suitable glues or adhesives.
- Timber-based materials:
  - 3 mm MDF and balsa wood are often used when a more robust model is required.
  - These materials are more expensive than card, but still relatively cheap and easy to source.

Card can be cut accurately using a craft knife

Polystyrene block is suitable for making solid concept models

- Timber-based materials require specialist cutting equipment, such as tenon saws, coping saws and vibrating fret saws (also known as scroll saws).
- Adhesives, panel pins and hot glue guns can be used to join pieces together.

Thin MDF can be used where a more robust model is needed

Toiles

- **Toiles** are widely used in the textiles and fashion industry.
- A toile is a test version of a piece of clothing made from cheap materials.
- They are made to check the effectiveness of a pattern that has been produced for a garment.
- This can then be evaluated and the pattern improved without wasting more expensive materials.

CAD Models

- On-screen 3D models can also be produced using computer-aided design (CAD) software.
- Models can be rotated and viewed from any angle.
- They are easy to edit and changes can be made quickly.
- They can be simulated to evaluate how they would respond to different conditions.
- As these are not physical models they cannot be handled. They can however be outputted to computer-aided manufacture (CAM) or rapid prototyping equipment to produce a physical piece (see pages 96 and 97).

> **Key Point**
>
> CAD software can be used to produce 3D models that can be simulated on screen.

A designer using CAD software to produce a 3D model

> **Quick Test**
>
> 1. Why do designers make models?
> 2. What materials are suitable for making models?
> 3. Why are toiles made?
> 4. What is a CAD model?

> **Key Words**
>
> model
> concept model
> toile

Wastage

You must be able to:

- Identify the tools used when wasting different materials
- Select an appropriate tool to waste a stated material and justify your choice.

Wastage

- Wastage, or wasting, is the removal of material.

Paper and boards

- Tools used for cutting paper and card include:
  - scalpels or craft knives: these are normally used with a safety ruler and a baseboard
  - compass cutters and circle cutters are used to cut circles in thin card
  - rotary trimmers and guillotines are used to make straight cuts in paper and card.
- Holes can be made by punching, using a punch or a die cutter.

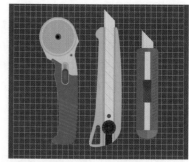
Rotary cutter and craft knives

Rotary trimmer

Timber

- The range of sawing tools used for cutting timber includes:
  - tenon saws: used for straight cuts in wood
  - coping saws, powered fretsaws and jigsaws: used for curved cuts in wood and thin plastic
  - band saws: used for straight and curved cuts in timber, plastic and thin sheet metal
  - circular saws: used for straight cuts in large pieces of wood or boards such as plywood or MDF (thin sheets of MDF or laser ply can be cut on a laser as well).
- Drilling makes holes by rotating a drill or boring bit clockwise as it is pushed into the material. Types of drill include portable power drills and pedestal drills (also known as pillar drills), which can be bench- or floor-mounted. It is important that the material is held firmly in place when drilling.
- Parts with a circular profile can be made by turning on a wood lathe. The tool is rested on a support and moved by hand.

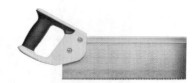
Tenon saw

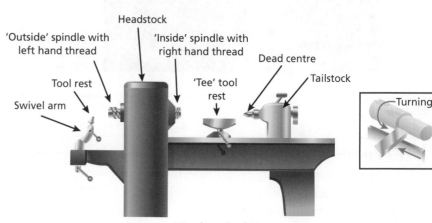

'Outside' spindle with left hand thread

Tool rest

Swivel arm

Headstock

'Inside' spindle with right hand thread

'Tee' tool rest

Dead centre

Tailstock

Turning

Wood-turning lathe

Metals

- Metal can be sawn by hand using a hacksaw or, for small pieces, a junior hacksaw. Thin sheet can be cut on a band saw and thicker pieces can be cut using a powered hacksaw.
- Drilling can be used to make holes, using portable power drills and pedestal drills.
- Shearing is used to cut thin metal sheet, using tin snips or a guillotine. The force applied along the cutting edge literally pushes the metal apart.
- Turning metal is similar to turning wood, but is carried out using a centre lathe. The work piece is normally held in a chuck and rotated against a blade. The cutting tool can be moved left and right (*z* direction) and in or out (*x* direction). Lathes can also be used to cut internal or external threads.

Tin snips

Polymers

- Thin sheet polymers can be sawn using coping saws, powered fretsaws and band saws. Acrylic can be cut on a laser. Some materials should not be laser cut as they give off toxic fumes.
- Similar to timber and metals, holes can be drilled using portable power drills and pedestal drills.

Bench-top pedestal drill

Fibres and Fabrics

- Fabrics can be cut using a rotary cutter or sheared using scissors. Some can also be cut on a laser cutter.
- Pinking shears are a special type of scissor with a serrated edge, to prevent the fabric fraying.

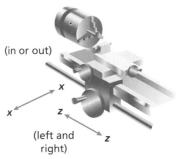

(in or out)

x

x   *z*

(left and right)   *z*

Centre lathe

Design Engineering

- Another wasting process used when making prototypes is etching. This involves removing a very small amount from the surface of a material, for example to engrave a logo. Etching can be achieved by heat using a laser cutter or by machining processes. Some materials can also be etched using corrosive chemicals.

Pinking shears

Key Point

The choice of wasting process depends on the material to be removed.

Quick Test

1. Name four tools used to cut thin card.
2. Name three types of saw that could be used to make a curved cut in thin plastic.
3. What is the difference between normal scissors and pinking shears?

Key Words

wasting
punching
turning
shearing
etching

Additive Manufacturing Processes

You must be able to:

- Identify the processes used to join a range of materials
- Select an appropriate tool to join a stated material and justify your choice.

Addition Processes

- Addition processes involve adding material to a product. This may involve joining materials together or adding layers by laminating.

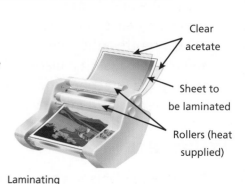

Clear acetate

Sheet to be laminated

Rollers (heat supplied)

Laminating

Paper and Boards

- One of the simplest methods to permanently join paper and board is using adhesives, such as:
  - polyvinyl acetate (PVA), either as liquid or in glue sticks
  - aerosol adhesive, also called spray mount
  - glue guns, which use heated polymers.
- Laminating involves adding layers of material, which makes a composite; for example, using heat to enclose paper or card between two layers of plastic. Takeaway food containers can also be laminated products, made from card with layers of aluminium foil and clear polymer.

Timber

- Timber parts can be permanently attached together using PVA adhesive.
- To increase the contact area, and therefore strength, of the joint different arrangements of wood joint can be used. The more complicated a joint is, the more effort will be needed to make it. Joints can be reinforced using nails or panel pins.

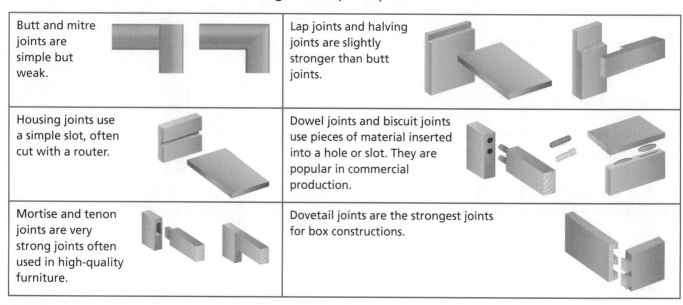

Butt and mitre joints are simple but weak.	Lap joints and halving joints are slightly stronger than butt joints.
Housing joints use a simple slot, often cut with a router.	Dowel joints and biscuit joints use pieces of material inserted into a hole or slot. They are popular in commercial production.
Mortise and tenon joints are very strong joints often used in high-quality furniture.	Dovetail joints are the strongest joints for box constructions.

- Screws can be used to make temporary joints.
- Another addition process used with timber products is laminating. This involves sticking together layers of material. For example, an expensive wood can be attached to the surface of a manufactured board to improve its appearance. Alternatively a plastic surface can be applied for protection, for example on a kitchen worktop.

Metals

- Metals can be joined together or to other materials using an epoxy resin type of adhesive. However, the joint is much weaker than the metal.
- Welding uses heat to melt the edges of the metals being joined, normally with extra added 'filler' metal. When the melted metals cool they form the joint. The heat can be from a flame or an electric arc.
- Brazing is carried out at a lower temperature than welding and the metal parts being joined do not melt. It involves melting a filler metal to form the joint.
- Riveting involves drilling a hole through two metal sheets and pushing a rivet through. The blank end is then hammered to form a second head, which holds the material in place. Pop rivets are fitted using a gun from one side of the material.

Polymers

- Solvent cement is a type of adhesive that only works with polymers. It dissolves the surface of the polymer parts so that they can mix together and form a joint as they solidify.
- Heat can be used to melt the edges of thermoplastics, forming a joint as they cool. The heat can be provided by contact against an electrically heated welding gun or hot plate.

Fibres and Fabrics

- Sewing with thread is the most common method of joining fabrics.
- Bonding uses a strip of adhesive web placed between the fabrics to be joined. Heat from an iron then fuses them together.
- As well as bonding, adhesives can be used to laminate fabrics.

Design Engineering

- When making electronic circuits, the components are typically joined to the circuit board by soldering. This involves melting solder to form the joint between the component and the circuit board.

Welding a steel pipe

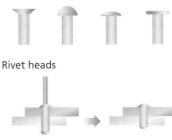
Rivet heads

Rivet inserted from one side → Pin snaps off, swelling head on underside

Fitting a pop rivet

Soldering

Key Words

laminating
welding
brazing
sewing
bonding
soldering

Quick Test

1. Name six different types of wood joint.
2. Explain the differences between welding and brazing.
3. Describe how two pieces of fabric can be bonded together.

Deforming and Reforming

You must be able to:

- Identify the processes used to deform or reform a range of materials
- Select an appropriate tool to deform or reform a stated material and justify your choice.

Deforming and Reforming

- Deforming and reforming processes involve changing the shape of a material without the gain or loss of material.

Paper and Boards

- Accurate folds can be achieved in cardboard by creasing the material first, using a creasing bar. This keeps the strength of the material, whereas scoring weakens it.
- A perforation cutter makes a row of small holes in paper or card so that a part can be torn off easily.

Timber

- Strips of timber can be bent by heating them in steam until they become pliable. They can then be shaped round a former. The wood must be clamped in place until it is cool.
- Curved shapes can also be made by gluing thin strips of wood together and clamping them against a former until the glue dries.

Metal-plate bending machine

Metals

- Bars and pipes can be bent round a former. The bar might be heated to make it easier to bend.
- Metal plates can be curved by feeding them between rollers moving at different speeds. The more times this is repeated, the smaller the radius of the curve.
- Folds and bends in sheet metal can be made using a press. Pressing is the application of pressure to deform a material.
- Casting can be used to make 3D products from metal. It involves pouring molten metal into a mould where it cools. Any waste material can be re-melted and used again.
- Sand casting is used to cast aluminium and cast iron.
  - The mould is made using a pattern. This is sandwiched between two boxes of sand, called a cope and drag.
  - Once sand is compressed around the pattern, the cope and drag are carefully separated and the pattern removed, leaving a hollow shape.

Casting molten aluminium into moulds

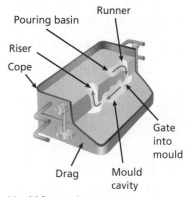

Mould for sand casting

- There will also be holes for a runner, to allow the metal to be poured in, and a riser, to let air escape.
- When the cope and drag are put back together the liquid metal can be poured in.

Polymers

- Simple bends can be made in thermoplastics by **line bending**. This heats just the area where the bend is needed until it is flexible. The plastic can then be held against a former or jig until it cools.
- 3D products can be made using **moulding** processes. For example:
  - Press or yoke moulding: plastic sheet is heated in an oven until it is flexible. It is then pressed between a mould and a yoke (also known as a male and female mould, respectively). Once cooled, it retains the shape of the mould.
  - In **vacuum forming**, the pressure pushing the heated plastic onto the mould comes from the atmosphere, when the air between the mould and plastic is sucked out.

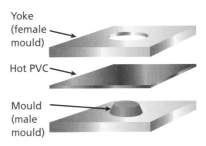

Yoke (female mould)

Hot PVC

Mould (male mould)

Yoke moulding

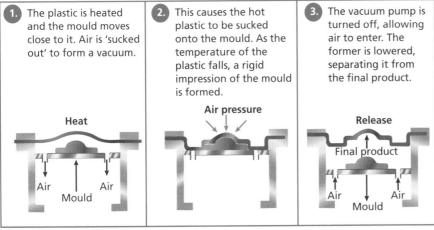

| 1. The plastic is heated and the mould moves close to it. Air is 'sucked out' to form a vacuum. | 2. This causes the hot plastic to be sucked onto the mould. As the temperature of the plastic falls, a rigid impression of the mould is formed. | 3. The vacuum pump is turned off, allowing air to enter. The former is lowered, separating it from the final product. |

Heat — Air — Air — Mould

Air pressure

Release — Final product — Air — Air — Mould

Vacuum-forming process

Key Point

The choice of process to change the shape depends on the material.

Fibres and Fabrics

- Shape can be added to textile garments by pressing and adding creases with an iron.
- **Gathering** allows a garment to increase fullness or widen out. It uses a sewing technique to allow a longer piece of fabric to be attached within the length of a shorter piece.
- **Pleating** is a type of gathering in which the folds are larger. It usually involves making a double or multiple fold in a textile product, held by stitching at the top or side.

Pleated skirt

Key Words

perforation
pressing
casting
line bending
moulding
vacuum forming
gathering
pleating

Quick Test

1. State two ways of making a curved shape from flat timber.
2. Name three processes used to form shapes from sheets of thermoplastic.
3. Describe how to put a pleat in a garment.

Ensuring Accuracy

You must be able to:

- Explain the reasons why accuracy is important when manufacturing products and prototypes
- Describe how jigs, templates and patterns are used to ensure accuracy
- Explain the importance of tolerances when manufacturing products.

Why Accuracy is Important

- **Accuracy** is extremely important when manufacturing products and prototypes.
- The design specification and related drawings will give the measurements and dimensions required for the product. Just a small deviation from these can result in a product that is not fit for purpose.
- For example, if a product has two parts that must be fitted together and the distance between the holes for fasteners is wrong, it would need to be remade. This would take extra time, meaning deadlines might not be met. It would also cost extra money in terms of labour and materials.

Tools that Improve Accuracy

- There is a wide range of tools that can be used to ensure accuracy. The main tools used in design and technology applications are jigs, templates and patterns.
- The increase in the use of computer-aided manufacture (CAM; see pages 96 and 97) and computer numerical control (CNC; see pages 100 and 101) equipment means that jigs, templates and patterns are not as widely used as they once were, but they are still important aids when manufacturing by hand.

Jigs

- **Jigs** are custom-made tools designed to achieve accuracy, repeatability and interchangeability during product manufacture.
- They are used to ensure that parts of a product are made exactly the same, without the need for marking out.
- For example, use of a jig can ensure that holes are drilled in exactly the same place on different pieces of wood.
- Printed circuit board (PCB) jigs can be used to test for faults in an electronic circuit.

Templates

- **Templates** are used to draw a shape onto material which can then be cut around.
- They are particularly useful when a large number of complex identical shapes have to be cut.

> **Key Point**
>
> Accuracy during manufacture is important to ensure that a product is fit for purpose.

Computer numerical control (CNC) equipment

> **Key Point**
>
> The increased use of computer numerical control (CNC) equipment has reduced the need for jigs and templates, but they are still important.

Patterns

- **Patterns** are a type of template that is widely used in the textiles industry.
- They are used to trace the parts of a garment onto fabric before it is cut.
- They are usually made from paper, but can be made from sturdier materials such as cardboard if they are to be used repeatedly.
- Clothing manufacturers usually employ specialist pattern makers as it is a highly skilled job.

Tolerance

- **Tolerance** is the permissible limits of variation in the dimensions or physical properties of a manufactured product or part.
- Manufacturers need tolerance information so that they understand the importance of the dimensions or measurements that they have been given.
- Failure to consider tolerances can lead to improper fits, wasted materials and the additional cost of remaking a product or part.

Minimising Waste

- When cutting materials, it is important to minimise the amount of waste that is created.
- Wasting less material leads to reduced costs and is better for the environment. For example, using less timber-based material means that fewer trees need to be cut down. Using less plastic means less oil needs to be found and extracted.
- Techniques for minimising waste when cutting include:
  - Shapes to be cut should be marked out so that the gaps between them are as small as possible.
  - Using good sawing technique can help to ensure that materials are cut accurately and to a good standard.
  - Any off-cuts can be placed in a separate bin. These can then be reused where appropriate instead of selecting fresh material.

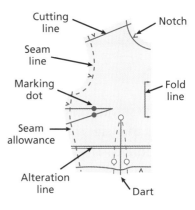

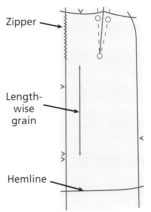

An example of a pattern used in clothing manufacture

Key Point

Taking tolerances into account reduces the likelihood of improper fits of manufactured parts.

Key Words

accuracy
jig
template
pattern
tolerance

Quick Test

1. Why is accuracy important during manufacture?
2. What is the main purpose of a jig?
3. What is meant by tolerance in product manufacture?
4. How can waste be minimised when cutting materials?

Digital Design Tools

You must be able to:

- Explain the advantages and disadvantages of using CAD and CAM
- Describe the main applications of CAE and rapid prototyping.

CAD

- CAD stands for **computer-aided design**.
- It is the use of computer software to produce designs for products. These can be 2D drawings or 3D models.

Advantages of CAD

- CAD is extremely accurate, often more accurate than drawing designs by hand.
- It is easier to modify or revise an existing design.
- 3D models can be rotated and viewed from different angles.
- Designs can be simulated to see how well they will function. This allows potential problems to be spotted early.
- Designs can be exported to CAM equipment for manufacture.

Disadvantages of CAD

- Some CAD packages are expensive to buy, so there can be high initial setup costs.
- There needs to be access to appropriate information and computing technology (ICT) hardware to run the software. This usually needs to be a computer with a very good specification, which adds to the cost.
- Some designers may not be familiar with how to use CAD software, so time and money must be spent training them. They must also update their skills regularly.

A designer using CAD software

CAM

- CAM stands for **computer-aided manufacture**.
- It is the use of computer software to control machine tools to manufacture products.
- Examples of CAM equipment include lasers cutters, vinyl cutters and 3D plotters.

Advantages of CAM

- Complex shapes can be produced much more easily than when manufacturing by hand.
- There is consistency of manufacture as every product is produced exactly the same.
- It enables very high levels of manufacturing accuracy.

> ### Key Point
>
> CAD and CAM improve accuracy of design and manufacture, but often involve high initial setup costs.

- There is greater efficiency as machines can run 24 hours a day, 7 days a week.
- It can increase the speed of manufacture, especially when producing products in large numbers.

Disadvantages of CAM

- As with CAD, initial setup costs can be high. CAM machines are usually very expensive, although their cost is reducing with time.
- Operators must be trained to use the equipment, which adds time and cost.
- For one-off products, CAM can actually be slower than if the product was produced by hand.

A laser cutter in operation

CAE

- CAE stands for computer-aided engineering.
- It is the use of computer software to aid in engineering analysis tasks. For example, analysing the robustness of a manufactured product or component.
- It is widely used in a range of industries, such as aviation, shipbuilding and car manufacture.

Rapid Prototyping

- Rapid prototyping is the processes and techniques used to quickly produce a product or component directly from CAD data.
- It is usually used to produce a prototype that can be used for evaluation purposes, rather than a finished product.
- 3D printing is a common example of a rapid prototyping process. This works by building up layers and layers of material to create a solid 3D form.

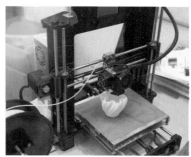

A 3D printer in operation

Image Creation Software

- Designers also make use of image creation and manipulation software.
- For example, this software can be used when preparing images of a product prototype for a presentation to stakeholders.

 Key Point

Rapid prototyping can be used to quickly create a product prototype that can be evaluated by stakeholders.

 Key Words

computer-aided design (CAD)
computer-aided manufacture (CAM)
computer-aided engineering (CAE)
rapid prototyping

Quick Test

1. What is meant by the terms CAD, CAM and CAE?
2. What are the advantages of CAD?
3. What are the advantages of CAM?
4. What is rapid prototyping used for?

Scales of Manufacture

You must be able to:

- Describe the characteristics and give examples of different scales of manufacture
- Describe approaches used to improve manufacturing efficiency
- Explain how new and emerging technologies are influencing manufacturing.

Scales of Manufacture

- Scale of manufacture is about the number of identical products to be made.
- As the quantity of products to be made increases, the processes to be carried out, such as wasting or joining, may be the same; however, the tools and equipment used to carry out these processes may be different.

Key Point

The quantity of products to be made has a significant effect on the equipment selected to manufacture the products.

Type	Characteristics	Example
One-off/ bespoke production	• One product is made at a time. • This could be a prototype or an object made for a specific customer. • Tools and equipment are used to make many different products. • It usually takes a long time for each product, a high level of worker skill and the cost of each product is high.	A tailored suit for a customer, satellites
Batch production	• A group of identical products are made together. • Once completed, another group of similar (but not necessarily identical) products may be made using the same equipment. • Some processes may be automated. Dedicated jigs might be used.	Furniture: tables, chairs
Mass production	• Very large quantities of identical products are needed. • The product typically goes through different processes on a production line. • The equipment is only used to make the same products, again and again. Most processes are automated with dedicated jigs and fixtures. • The cost per product is low compared to other methods.	Chocolate bars, cars, nuts and bolts

Improving Manufacturing Efficiency

- Manufacturers typically have access to tools and equipment that are similar to those of their competitors. How effectively they use this equipment determines whether they get a competitive advantage.

- **Lean manufacturing** is an approach that aims to make products in the most effective and efficient way possible. Lean manufacturing involves eliminating all forms of waste during manufacturing. Waste here is not referring just to rubbish or removed material: it refers to any activity that does not add value to the product. For example, waste includes:
  - moving products around a factory
  - time workers spend looking for tools
  - making too many products
  - doing more to the product than the customer needs
  - making defective parts.
- Typically, most manufacturers have a stock of materials waiting to be processed. This is a waste as stock costs money, which is tied up in the company. With **just-in-time manufacturing**, suppliers deliver materials only when they are needed. This means less money is tied up in materials. However, if suppliers don't deliver on time or there are quality problems, this can stop production, meaning that expensive equipment is standing around unused.

Impact of New and Emerging Technologies

- An increase in the quantity of products to be made can give opportunities for **economies of scale**. For example, if someone cuts one shape from card, they may use scissors. If 1000 of the same shape must be cut, a laser cutter or a die cutter might be used; the equipment costs more but cuts faster, meaning the total cost per product can be less.
- **Disruptive technologies** are innovations that create a new way of doing things. These can mean that the process used to make products can be changed significantly. For example:
  - Robotic systems can be used to carry out manufacturing operations, load machines and assemble products.
  - 3D printing enables a complex product to be made in a single operation, where several complex machines may have been needed previously. Further, the printers could be installed in people's homes, rather than making products in factories.

A robot arm packaging products

3D printing

> **Key Point**
>
> Disruptive technologies are innovations that allow new ways of making products.

> **Key Words**
>
> one-off/bespoke
>   production
> batch production
> mass production
> lean manufacturing
> just-in-time
>   manufacturing
> economies of scale
> disruptive technology

Quick Test

1. Give two examples of products that are mass produced.
2. State one drawback of just-in-time manufacturing.
3. Name two disruptive technologies.

Large-Scale Processes: Paper, Timber and Metals

You must be able to:

- Describe manufacturing processes used for larger scales of production with papers and board
- Describe manufacturing processes used for larger scales of production with timber
- Describe manufacturing processes used for larger scales of production with metals.

Paper and Boards

- **Offset lithography** works on the principle that grease and water don't mix. The image to print is in relief on the printing plate, which attracts grease (ink) applied to it. The plate is dampened, which repels ink off any non-image areas. The printing plate then transfers an inked image onto the rubber blanket cylinder, which in turn presses the image onto the paper or card as it is fed through.
- Screen printing, also known as screen process printing, uses simple stencils, which can each be used to apply a single colour. It is used to quickly produce cheap prints on T shirts and banners.
- Digital printing means the whole design and printing process is carried out by a computer.
- Vinyl cutters are **computer numerical controlled (CNC)** machines that use a blade to plot and cut shapes in self-adhesive vinyl. The shape can then be peeled off and stuck where desired.
- **Die cutting** is used to cut shapes and holes. It uses metal blades which can cut a complete net in a single operation. Creases can be marked using a blunt blade. Foam rubber around the blade compresses during cutting and pushes to release the cut material.

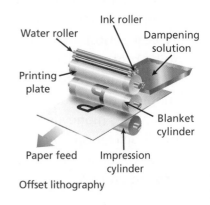

Offset lithography

Screen printing

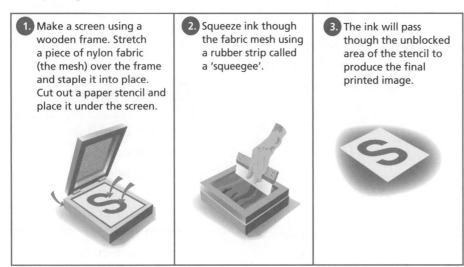

1. Make a screen using a wooden frame. Stretch a piece of nylon fabric (the mesh) over the frame and staple it into place. Cut out a paper stencil and place it under the screen.

2. Squeeze ink though the fabric mesh using a rubber strip called a 'squeegee'.

3. The ink will pass though the unblocked area of the stencil to produce the final printed image.

Vinyl cutter

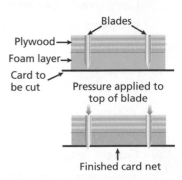

Die cutting

Timber

- CNC routers are used to make grooves and edge profiles. They use computer-controlled stepper motors to move the router and are very common in the furniture industry and school workshops.
- Band saws and circular saws (see page 88) are used to cut timber.
- Steam bending machines heat timber in steam until it becomes pliable. It can then be shaped around a former.
- CNC versions of wood lathes (see page 88) are used to make turned parts and bowls.

Metals

- CNC milling uses a rotating tool to make flats or grooves in metal. Computer-controlled stepper motors can move the workpiece in the x and y directions, and the tool in the z direction.
- CNC versions of metal lathes (see page 89) are used to turn round parts.
- Sheet metal can be folded using a press which forces the metal against an angled former to bend it.
- Presses are also used to bend and form sheet metal and stamp out holes. The presses use massive pressure from hydraulic rams, to make products such as car body panels.
- Unlike sand casting (see page 92), die casting uses a reusable metal mould. Molten metal is poured into a cylinder. A ram then forces this metal into the mould, holding pressure until it has cooled. The mould is then opened and the component removed.

Milling machine

> **Key Point**
>
> Industrial manufacturing processes carry out the same tasks as manual tools, but typically with computer control and reusable moulds or formers. This allows them to operate much faster.

Metal folding	Pressing	Die casting
	Pressure from hydraulic press — Final product. Punch, Sheet metal, Die	Molten metal, Crucible, Split mould, Ram, Hydraulic system

> **Quick Test**
>
> 1. Name two processes used to print paper and board.
> 2. Name one industrial application of CNC routers.
> 3. What is the mould in die casting made from?

> **Key Words**
>
> offset lithography
> computer numerical control (CNC)
> die cutting
> die casting

Large-Scale Processes: Polymers and Fabrics

You must be able to:

- Describe manufacturing processes used for larger scales of production with polymers
- Describe manufacturing processes used for larger scales of production with fibres and fabrics
- Describe manufacturing processes used for larger scales of production with design engineering.

Polymers

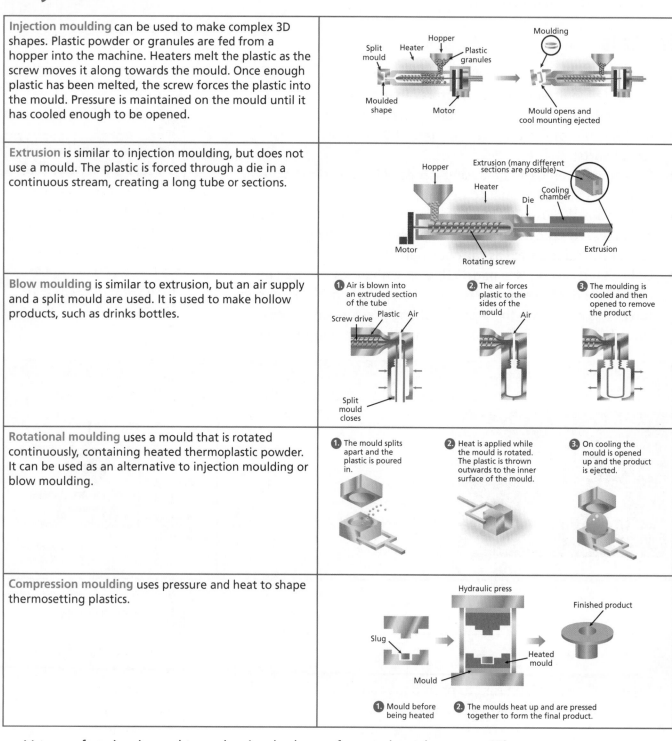

Injection moulding can be used to make complex 3D shapes. Plastic powder or granules are fed from a hopper into the machine. Heaters melt the plastic as the screw moves it along towards the mould. Once enough plastic has been melted, the screw forces the plastic into the mould. Pressure is maintained on the mould until it has cooled enough to be opened.	
Extrusion is similar to injection moulding, but does not use a mould. The plastic is forced through a die in a continuous stream, creating a long tube or sections.	
Blow moulding is similar to extrusion, but an air supply and a split mould are used. It is used to make hollow products, such as drinks bottles.	
Rotational moulding uses a mould that is rotated continuously, containing heated thermoplastic powder. It can be used as an alternative to injection moulding or blow moulding.	
Compression moulding uses pressure and heat to shape thermosetting plastics.	

- Vacuum forming is used to make simple shapes from a sheet (see page 93).

Fibres and Fabrics

Digital lay planning is the use of computer software to arrange a pattern on a material. The aim is to minimise the waste of material.

Band saws can be used to quickly cut a pattern into a stack of material.

Unlike domestic sewing machines, which are designed to be very flexible and carry out a wide range of tasks, industrial sewing machines are often designed to perform a specific type of stitch or carry out a specific task, such as making buttonholes or attaching buttons.

An overlocker is a specialised industrial sewing machine used to give seams and hems a professional finish or add decorative edgings.

Flat-bed and rotary screen printing apply colour to fabric that moves through the machine on a conveyor belt. In flat-bed printing, an automated squeegee applies ink through a screen as the fabric progresses in a series of starts. In rotary screen printing, the ink is applied by a series of rollers, and the fabric moves continuously.

Automated presses and steam dollies can be used to shape, stabilise and set textile materials rather than pressing or ironing by hand.

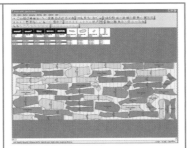
Digital lay planning

Overlocker

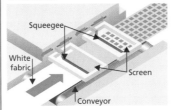
Flat-bed screen printing

Key Point

Most industrial polymer-moulding processes use reusable metal moulds.

Key Point

There is a wide variety of plastic-moulding processes: the optimum choice for an application depends on the design of the part being made.

Design Engineering

Laser cutting can be used to accurately and rapidly cut out 2D shapes from CAD drawings. These can be used to make models of products.

Industrial laser cutter

Rapid prototyping is a manufacturing technology used to produce a 3D product in a single operation from a CAD model. Types of rapid prototyping include 3D printing and stereolithography. The prototype is normally built up by adding layers of material, one at a time. Although it may be made from different materials to the final product, it can be used to check form and fit.

3D printing a prototype product from a CAD model

Key Point

Industrial manufacturing processes are often designed to repeat one task, over and over again. Computer control allows them to operate much faster than manual processes.

Key Words

injection moulding
extrusion
blow moulding
rotational moulding
compression moulding
overlocker

Quick Test

1. Name two industrial processes used to apply print to fabric.
2. Name a rapid prototyping process.

Review Questions

Technical Understanding

1 **a)** Complete the table below by entering a suitable electronic component to achieve each function. State whether each is an input or output.

Function	Component	Input or Output
Detect changes in light level		
Produce light		
Produce sound		
Detect that something has been moved		
Produce motion		

[10]

b) Finishing materials can improve their aesthetic qualities. Explain **one other** reason why materials are finished.

....

....

.... [2]

2 A fashion designer is designing a dress for a television presenter. This includes darts in the skirt.

a) Describe what is meant by darts.

....

....

....

.... [2]

b) Explain the purpose of darts in a textile product.

[2]

3 The figure shows a right-angled triangle. It is part of the reinforcement structure in a bridge. Calculate the length of side *b*.

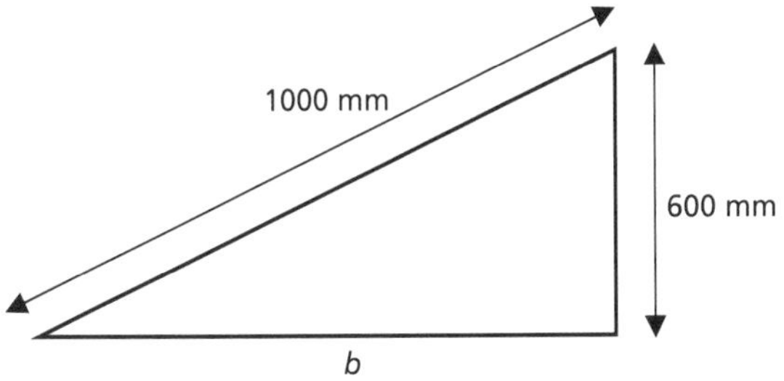

[3]

4 Identify the types of motion represented by each of the diagrams.

a) 	b) 
c) 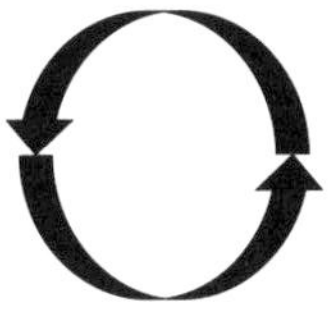	d) 

[4]

5. Complete the table, which lists how mechanical devices convert between types of motion. The first line has been completed as an example.

Device	Type of Motion Input	Type of Motion Output
Pulley	Rotary motion	Rotary motion
a)	Linear motion	Linear motion in opposite direction
Rack and pinion	b)	c)
Cam	Rotary	d)

[4]

6. A team of designers is developing an electric vehicle. To transfer the motion from the motor to the wheels they are considering using either pulleys and belts or two spur gears. Compare the advantages and disadvantages of these two approaches.

....

....

....

....

....

....

....

....

....

....

....

[6]

7 A design is being produced for a child's night light.

The night light must:

- Automatically detect when it has become dark

- Light up for a timed period after it has gone dark.

a) Give a suitable input and output device for the night light.

Input

....

Output

.... [2]

b) The designer has decided to use a programmable component as the process stage of the system.

Explain **two** reasons why this would be a good choice.

1. ....

....

....

....

2. ....

....

....

.... [4]

Total Marks .... / 39

Practice Questions

Manufacturing Processes and Techniques

1 **a)** Define the following terms.

Toile

....

....

....

....

Iterative design

....

....

....

.... [4]

b) Give **three** materials that can be used to produce an early model of a design.

1. ....

2. ....

3. .... [3]

2 **a)** State **two** tools that can be used to cut a fabric by hand.

1. .... [1]

2. .... [1]

b) Explain the purpose of 'gathering' when making a garment from fabric.

....

....

....

.... [2]

3 Identify the wood joints shown below. The first has been completed for you.

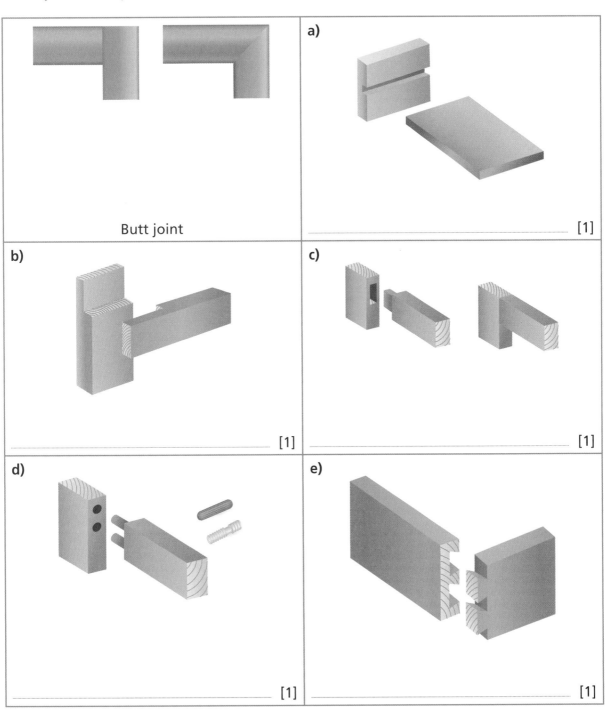

Butt joint

a) .... [1]

b) .... [1]

c) .... [1]

d) .... [1]

e) .... [1]

Practice Questions

4   Explain how accuracy can be ensured when manufacturing products. Use examples to support your answer.

[12]

5 The image shows a designer using CAD.

Give **three** advantages and **two** disadvantages of using CAD to design prototypes.

Advantage 1

_____

_____

Advantage 2

_____

_____

Advantage 3

_____

_____

Disadvantage 1

_____

_____

Disadvantage 2

_____

_____

[5]

Practice Questions

6. Explain how the scale of production affects the cost of a manufactured product.

[10]

7 Describe how die cutters are used to make products from card.

[3]

8 Give **two** uses of a CNC router.

1.

2. [2]

9 State what an overlocker is used for in textiles.

[1]

10 Describe how rotary screen printing is used in textile manufacturing.

[4]

Total Marks _____ / 53

Review Questions

Manufacturing Processes and Techniques

1 **a)** Explain **two** reasons why designers produce models of their designs.

1. ....

....

....

....

2. ....

....

....

.... [4]

b) Explain **two** reasons why card is a good material to use when producing early models of a design.

1. ....

....

....

....

2. ....

....

....

.... [4]

2 State adhesives that would typically be used to make each of the following joints.

a) Metal to metal.

.... [1]

b) Wood to wood.

.... [1]

c) Thermoplastic polymer to thermoplastic polymer.

.... [1]

3 Using notes and/or sketches, describe the process of press (yoke) moulding polymers.

[4]

4 State **two** methods that are used in design engineering to etch materials.

1. .... [1]

2. .... [1]

Review Questions

5 **a)** Define the following terms.

Jig

....

....

....

....

Tolerance

....

....

....

....

[4]

b) Explain why it is important to use tolerances when manufacturing products.

....

....

....

....

....

[3]

6 Give **three** advantages and **two** disadvantages of using CAM to produce prototypes.

Advantage 1

Advantage 2

Advantage 3

Disadvantage 1

Disadvantage 2

[5]

Review Questions

7   Give **two** examples of products that are typically made using each of the following scales of manufacture.

One-off production	Example 1	
	Example 2	
Batch production	Example 1	
	Example 2	
Mass production	Example 1	
	Example 2	

[6]

8   Describe how a product is made by die casting.

....

....

....

....

....

....

....

[4]

9 **a)** State what is meant by just-in-time manufacturing.

....

.... [1]

b) Explain **one** advantage and **one** disadvantage to a company of using just-in-time manufacturing.

Advantage

....

....

Disadvantage

....

.... [4]

10 Using notes and/or sketches, describe how a plastic bottle is made by blow moulding.

[4]

1. A design is being produced for a doorbell system. A programmable component is to be used to control how the system works.

The programmable system must:

- Detect when a switch has been pressed

- Activate a buzzer for a period of 5 seconds after the switch has been pressed

- Turn off the buzzer after the time period has ended

- Turn on an LED after the buzzer has stopped sounding.

Write a program that meets the needs of the doorbell system described above. You may use any programming language that you are familiar with.

[6]

2 **a)** Describe how energy is generated using fossil fuels.

[3]

b) What type of energy source is a fossil fuel?

[1]

c) Explain **one** advantage and **one** disadvantage of using nuclear fuel.

Advantage

Disadvantage

[4]

Mixed Exam-Style Questions

3　Explain in detail why designers explore existing products.
Use examples to support your answer.

_____

_____

_____

_____

_____

_____

_____

_____

_____

_____

_____

_____

_____

_____

_____

_____ [12]

4 **a)** Define the term CAD.

[2]

b) Define the term CAM.

[2]

c) Define the term CAE.

[2]

5 **a)** State the difference between a sketch and a drawing.

[1]

b) Define the term 'exploded drawing'.

[2]

c) Give **one** example of how **each** of the following types of communication could be used in design and technology:

Flow chart

....

.... [1]

Mathematical modelling

....

.... [1]

6 A manufacturer is making a plastic product using the injection moulding process.

a) Using notes and/or sketches, describe the injection moulding process.

[5]

b) The volume of plastic in one product is 2.4×10^{-5} m³. After making 20 000 products, the manufacturer finds that he has used 0.5 m³ of material.

Calculate the volume of material that has been lost as waste during the manufacturing process.

[2]

c) The manufacturer has calculated that the total cost of each product will be £6.40.

The selling price is £8.00. Calculate the percentage profit.

[2]

7 Describe how rivets are used to join two metal sheets together.

[3]

8   Using notes and/or sketches, describe how a product is made using sand casting.

[10]

9 Complete the table, which lists the mechanical devices that can be used to convert between different types of motion.

Type of Motion Input	Type of Motion Output	Device
Rotary	Rotary (at 90° to the original)	a)
Linear	Linear (in reverse)	b)
Rotary	Reciprocating	c)
Reciprocating	Oscillating	d)
Linear	Rotary	e)

[5]

10 State the meaning of the term 'plasticity'.

[1]

11 The product shown below is A6 in size (folded from A5) and includes tear-off tags indicated by the dotted lines. The material available to make it is A1 sheets of carton board.

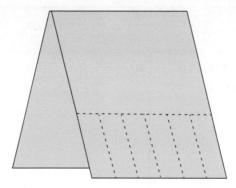

a) Describe the processes that would be used to make a prototype batch of 5 of the products.

_____

_____

_____

_____

_____

_____

_____

_____

_____

_____

[6]

b) The final product will be made in batches of 10 000. Identify a process that could be used to produce the net for the product in a single operation, so that it only needs to be folded.

_____

[1]

12 Choose one of the following products. Circle your selection.

Food packaging   **Flat-pack furniture**   **Electrical system in a fridge**

Plastic socket for an electric plug   **Fabric covering for a sofa**   **Metal hammer**

Discuss in detail the properties required by the product you have selected.

[9]

Total Marks _____ / 81

Answers

Page 9 Quick Test
1. Needs of user; where and how the product or system is to be used; social, cultural and economic factors.
2. So that their exact needs can be discussed.
3. Brief: short description of the design problem and how it is to be solved; specification: set of measurable criteria for the design.

Page 11 Quick Test
1. The design of products and systems that can be used by everyone (or as many people as possible).
2. Measurements that are taken from millions of people and put in charts. Used to ensure products are easy to use and interact with.
3. How a design or product appeals to the human senses.

Page 13 Quick Test
1. To gain ideas and inspiration and to learn from past successes and failures.
2. Materials, components, trends, marketing, usability, impact on society and the environment, and the work of past professionals.
3. A tool for systematically evaluating the environmental aspects of a product or system.
4. What can go wrong; what mistakes to avoid.

Page 15 Quick Test
1. Any change that makes a product better in some way.
2. A model that aims to increase the use of renewable energy and design products that are 'made to be made again'.
3. By changing how we act towards each other, such as how we communicate.

Page 17 Quick Test
1. They are burned to create steam. This then turns turbines, which drive the generators that produce electricity.
2. Solar, wind, hydro, tidal
3. They are clean, sustainable and will not run out.
4. To minimise energy losses from heat.

Page 19 Quick Test
1. Reduce, rethink, refuse, recycle, reuse, repair
2. Guaranteed minimum price for most products; Fairtrade Premium to spend on improving lifestyles.
3. To ensure any impacts are positive.

Page 21 Quick Test
1. Potential market, and cost of materials, components and manufacture.
2. The ability to advertise or promote the product.
3. They may withdraw funding or support if they think the product is not viable.

Pages 22–25 Design Considerations
1. a) For example: a person with an interest in a business [1], such as in the profits being made [1].
   b) Up to 3 marks for explanation. For example: stakeholders may have money invested in the project [1], so therefore have a right to some influence in the design brief created [1]. If the brief is not how they want it to be they may withdraw funding [1].
   c) Up to 3 marks for explanation. For example: if the country is in recession a company may not have as much money

to spend [1] on developing the design. This could lead to cheaper materials being chosen [1] which could affect the overall quality of the product [1].
2. a) 5–6 marks: thorough knowledge and understanding of the advantages and disadvantages of using renewable energy sources. All points fully explained. 3–4 marks: good knowledge and understanding of the advantages and disadvantages of using renewable energy sources. Majority of points explained. 1–2 marks: limited knowledge or understanding. Mainly descriptive response.

   Indicative answer: Renewable energy can replenish itself quickly whereas non-renewable energy cannot. Renewable energy produces far less carbon emissions than fossil fuels, resulting in less damage to the ozone layer. Renewable energy sources don't produce energy all of the time. For example, wind turbines only generate electricity when it is windy. This means that they may need to be supplemented with non-renewable sources. Some renewable energy sources, such as solar, have high setup and maintenance costs.
   b) 1 mark for each suitable response. For example: ergonomic considerations [1], aesthetic considerations [1].
   c) 1 mark for each suitable response. For example: nanoelectronics [1], smart materials [1].
3. a) Up to 2 marks for each description. For example: the materials that have been used [1] and how they impact on how the product works [1]. The influence of trends [1] and how this affects the popularity of products [1]. The impact on society [1] and how this affects wider groups of people [1].
   b) 1 mark for each suitable response. For example: cost/availability of materials [1], marketability of the product [1].
4. a) Up to 2 marks for explanation of each benefit. For example: guarantees a minimum price for most products [1] so that even if global prices fall producers will still get a fair price [1]. Producers receive Fairtrade Premium on top of their normal price [1], which they can then put towards improving their quality of life [1].
   b) Up to 2 marks for explanation. For example: might cost more to buy [1], which would make it unappealing for people on tight budgets [1].
   c) Up to 2 marks for definition of the term. For example: development that does not compromise the ability of future generations [1] to meet their own needs [1].
5. a) Green dot symbol [1]. Tells us that the manufacturer contributes to the cost of recycling [1].
   b) Mobius loop [1]. Shows us that a product can be recycled [1].
6. Reduce; rethink; refuse; recycle; reuse; repair [6]
7. Inclusive design is about designing products that can be used by (almost) everyone [1]. Exclusive design is when products are designed for a particular group of people [1].

Page 27 Quick Test
1. Freehand, crating, isometric projection
2. 30°
3. To make it look more realistic.

Page 29 Quick Test
1. It shows how the parts in a product fit together.
2. For example, any two of: calculating the values of components to use in an electrical circuit, designing the shape of speedboat hulls, determining how strong a bridge needs to be, simulating the testing of products.
3. A diamond

Answers

Page 31 Quick Test
1. A cyclic design approach where each iteration is tested, evaluated and refined, resulting in a new iteration.
2. Greater sense of user ownership in the final product; constant user feedback.
3. When designing electronic, mechanical or mechatronic systems.

Pages 32–35 Review Questions

Pages 32–35 Design Considerations
1. a) 5–6 marks: thorough knowledge and understanding of how new and emerging technologies impact on the development of design solutions. All points fully explained. 3–4 marks: good knowledge and understanding of how new and emerging technologies impact on the development of design solutions. Majority of points explained. 1–2 marks: limited knowledge or understanding. Mainly descriptive response.

    Indicative answer: New and emerging technologies allow new products and systems to be designed that were previously not possible. This results in problems being solved that previously could not be. This could include designs that improve people's lives and lifestyles. For example, nanotechnology is being developed that could improve the delivery of medicine for sick people in hospitals. New technologies can allow products to be designed in a more sustainable/environmentally friendly way. For example, bioplastics could be used to replace non-biodegradable carrier bags, thus producing less landfill waste.
    b) 1 mark for any suitable response. For example: the materials/processes/components that have been used [1].
    c) 1 mark for any suitable response. For example: where/how the product/system is to be used [1].
2. a) 1 mark for definition of the term. For example: the design of products that are accessible to/useable by as many people as possible [1].
    b) Up to 2 marks. For example: measurements taken from millions of people [1] and put together in charts [1].
    c) Up to 3 marks for explanation. For example: check charts showing head circumferences [1]. This would assist in creating appropriate sizes for the helmet design [1] so that it would properly fit a large number of firefighters [1].
    d) 1 mark for any suitable response. For example: it will determine whether the product will be commercially successful [1].
3. 5 marks for who, what, where, when and why.
4. a) 1 mark for each non-renewable source, such as fossil fuels and nuclear.
    b) 1 mark for each renewable source other than wind, such as solar and hydro.
    c) Up to 2 marks for explanation of advantage and 2 marks for explanation of disadvantage. For example: Advantage: better for the environment than using fossil fuels [1] as it does not release harmful greenhouse gases into the atmosphere [1]. Disadvantage: will not generate electricity when there is no wind [1] which means it is limited for use on products that will be placed in windy areas [1].
5. a) Up to 2 marks for definition of the term. For example: design that considers people's beliefs/principles/morals [1] and works to ensure that they are not compromised [1].
    b) Up to 2 marks for explanation of each way. For example: make the product easy to disassemble [1] so that the materials/components could be reused in a different product [1]. Make use of biodegradable materials [1] so that the product can be disposed of sustainably [1]. Make the product easy to repair [1] so it does not have to be thrown away when a component fails [1].

Pages 36–37 Practice Questions

Pages 36–37 Communicating Design Ideas
1. A 2D drawing is produced [1] either manually and scanned [1] or using a mouse/drawing tablet [1]. This is then processed by CAD software which turns it into a 3D drawing [1].
2. Award marks as follows, up to a maximum of 6 marks. To demonstrate how a system works [1], for example simulating the operation of a mechanical product [1]. To demonstrate how a system will change if modified [1], for example showing how changing components in an electrical circuit will change the outputs [1]. To provide data allowing a product to be designed for optimum performance [1], for example the shape of a speedboat hull [1]. To simulate the testing of a product or system [1], for example seeing how a bridge or structure will deform when a load is placed on it [1]. Any other relevant point [1].
3. Up to 2 marks for explanation of each benefit. For example: Iterative design: each iteration of the design is fully tested/evaluated [1], making it more likely that problems will be discovered early in the design process [1]. User-centred design: it fully considers the needs of the end user at all stages of the design process [1], making it more likely that they will be happy with the finished product [1]. Systems-based approach: it provides a top-down overview of the design [1], which is easy to explain/communicate to clients/stakeholders [1].
4. Isometric projection [1]

Pages 38–55 Revise Questions

Page 39 Quick Test
1. Tensile strength is resistance to a pulling force whereas compressive strength is resistance to a squeezing force.
2. Density, strength to weight ratio, thermal conductivity, electrical conductivity
3. When the force applied to a material is removed, elasticity means the material will return to its original shape whereas plasticity means that it will keep its deformed shape.

Page 41 Quick Test
1. Functionality (mechanical and physical properties), aesthetic, cost, environmental, social, cultural, ethical
2. Visual, tactile, aural, taste, smell
3. For example, whether workers involved in production are treated in a fair way, such as use of underage or poorly paid labour, or poor or unsafe working conditions.

Page 43 Quick Test
1. Bleached card
2. Grams per square metre, which indicates the thickness of paper or card.
3. Recycled paper cannot be used in products for food packaging.

Page 45 Quick Test
1. For example, oak, birch, teak
2. Planed square edge
3. MDF, plywood, blockboard

Page 47 Quick Test
1. A mixture of two or more metals
2. Any three of: stainless steel, brass, pewter, solder
3. Any four of: sheet, plate, bar (round or square), tube (round or square), ingots

Page 49 Quick Test
1. Carbon-based fossil fuels
2. Liquid resins and powders
3. Examples: ropes, carpets, packaging

Answers

Page 51 Quick Test
1. Knitted, woven, non-woven
2. Cotton, wool, silk
3. Oil

Page 53 Quick Test
1. Carbon
2. Less than 100 nm (nanometres)
3. Any three of: glass-reinforced polyester (GRP), fibreglass, carbon-reinforced polyester (CRP), reinforced concrete

Page 55 Quick Test
1. Hinges
2. Gears, cams, pulleys, belts, levers, linkages

Pages 56–57 Review Questions

Pages 56–57 Communicating Design Ideas
1. Up to 2 marks for explanation of each application. For example:
   a) 2D or 3D sketches: producing early ideas for designs [1] so they can be evaluated by stakeholders [1].
   b) Exploded drawings: showing how the parts of a product will fit together [1] to aid in the manufacture/assembly of the product [1].
   c) Flow charts: producing an order of operations for manufacture [1] so that workers can complete manufacture of the product efficiently/on time [1].
2. 9–12 marks: thorough knowledge and understanding of the importance of collaboration across material areas when designing solutions. Balanced discussion that comes to an appropriate, qualified conclusion. Several relevant examples presented to support answer. 5–8 marks: good knowledge and understanding of the importance of collaboration across material areas when designing solutions. Some balance to the discussion but focuses overly on advantages or disadvantages. Conclusion made but may not be qualified. Some relevant examples presented to support answer. 1–4 marks: limited knowledge or understanding. Mainly descriptive response and lack of balance. No conclusion. Few or no relevant examples presented to support answer.

   Indicative answer: Designs can be produced using a range of different material areas as appropriate to the problems faced. Collaboration ensures better shared knowledge of these material areas. Lack of collaboration may lead to potential opportunities for use of these material areas being missed. Specialists in different materials will carry expertise in understanding their properties. This can ensure that they are used appropriately in a design. For example, when designing a child's toy it may be necessary to call on plastics, textiles and electronics specialists to ensure that the product is fit for purpose. Too much input from others could cause disagreements on the direction of the design. A single designer may be able to complete the design more quickly and maintain better focus on the intended outcome.

Pages 58–63 Practice Questions

Pages 58–63 Material Considerations
1. a) Hardness [1]
   b) Thermal conductivity [1]
   c) Flammability [1]
2. a) Award 1 mark each for two suitable examples, for example based on fashion or customer preference for either political, religious or ethical reasons.
   b) Award marks as follows up to a maximum of 4 marks.

Using an irregular/non-stock form of the material can be very expensive [1] as this may have to be made especially for the product [1]. The closer the design to the size/shape of the stock form, the less machining will be needed [1], which means less waste [1] and lower overall cost for materials and machining [1]. Any other relevant point.

3. Award marks as indicated, with up to 2 marks for each characteristics box and 1 mark for each typical use box.

Type	Characteristics	Typical Use
Layout and tracing paper	Hard [1] and translucent [1] Typically 50–90 gsm [1]	For example working drawings [1], tracing [1]
Bleached card	Strong [1], white [1] Made from pure bleached wood pulp [1] 200–400 gsm [1]	For example book covers [1], expensive packaging [1]
Corrugated cardboard	Contains two or more layers of card with interlacing fluted inner section [1] Often made from recycled material [1], low cost [1] From 250 gsm upwards [1]	For example boxes [1], packaging [1]
Foil-lined board	Made by laminating aluminium foil to one side of another board [1]. Insulating properties [1], can keep moisture in/out [1]	For example drinks cartons [1], ready-meal lids [1]
Polypropylene sheet	Thermoplastic polymer [1] Low density [1], tough [1], flexible [1] and water resistant [1] From 30 μm (micrometres) thick upwards [1]	For example packaging [1] and labelling [1]

4. a) i) 1 mark for an appropriate answer, for example pine, cedar, spruce. [1]
      ii) 1 mark for a typical application of that softwood. For example (pine) construction work, joinery, furniture, (cedar) lining drawers and chests, fencing, (spruce) general construction, wooden aircraft frames.
      iii) 1 mark each for identifying a requirement of the application and justifying the choice with respect to one of the material properties (for example strength, weight, resistance to decay, aesthetics).
   b) i) 1 mark for an appropriate answer, for example oak, birch, teak, balsa. [1]
      ii) 1 mark for a typical application of that hardwood. For example (oak) high-quality furniture, (birch) furniture and cabinets, turned items, (teak) outdoor furniture, marine/boat fittings, (balsa) modelling.
      iii) 1 mark each for identifying a requirement of the application and justifying the choice with respect to one of the material properties (for example strength, weight, ability to be worked, resistance to moisture, aesthetics).
5. 1 mark each for any two of: rough sawn planks, PSE planks, mouldings.
6. Award up to 4 marks as follows (information can be conveyed either by sketches or notes): metal ore is mined or quarried [1]. The metal is extracted using heat [1], chemical reactions [1] or electrolysis [1]. The metals are then usually melted [1] and either cast into products [1] or mechanically shaped [1].

Answers

7. **a)** Non-ferrous [1]
   b) Any suitable application [1]
   c) Stainless steel [1]
   d) Copper [1]
   e) Any one of: low friction, corrosion resistant, malleable [1]
   f) Any one of: locks, bearings, musical instruments [1]
8. **a)** Any one of: silicone, epoxy resin, polyester resin, urea formaldehyde, melamine formaldehyde [1]
   b) Any typical application [1]
   c, e) Any one of: PET, HDPE, LDPE, PVC, PS, HIPS, PP, ABS, PMMA, TPE [1]
   d, f) Any typical application [1]
9. Award up to 4 marks as follows: a thermoplastic polymer softens when heated [1] and can be reshaped [1], whereas the form of a thermosetting polymer does not change with temperature [1] and when heated it may start to char. In a thermosetting polymer the polymer chains are permanently interlinked with chemical bonds [1].
10. Award up to 4 marks as follows (information can be conveyed either by sketches or notes):
    * Knitted fabrics are made from interlocking loops [1] whereas woven fabrics are constructed from interlocking yarns [1].
    * Knitted fabrics have greater elasticity than woven fabrics [1].
    * Woven fabrics have a grain due to the direction of the threads [1] and a selvedge (an edge that will not fray when cut) [1].
    * Any other relevant point.
11. **a)** Award up to 4 marks as follows: it is made from carbon atoms [1] arranged hexagonally in a flat 2D layer just one atom thick [1]. It is about 200 times stronger than steel [1], flexible [1], transparent [1] and conducts heat and electricity well [1].
    b) Award 1 mark each for up to three suitable applications; for example solar cells [1], touch panels [1] and smart windows for phones [1].
12. Award 1 mark each for any two of: resistors, capacitors, diodes/LEDs, transistors, microcontrollers, switches, motors.

Pages 64–75 Revise Questions

Page 65 Quick Test
1. To improve function or aesthetics.
2. A material that is already manufactured with a good surface finish.
3. Polishing

Page 67 Quick Test
1. To reduce cost, to reduce weight, to improve strength and rigidity
2. Triangles
3. Two from: boning, adding darts, layering

Page 69 Quick Test
1. Both move back and forwards, but reciprocating motion is in a straight line whereas oscillating motion swings down and up.
2. Rigid bar, fulcrum, load and effort
3. Third-class lever

Page 71 Quick Test
1. Rotary to reciprocating motion
2. Spur, bevel, worm and worm wheel, rack and pinion
3. It would make the pulley wheels run in opposite directions.

Page 73 Quick Test
1. Input, process, driver and output.
2. They have a resistance that varies depending on the light level.
3. Light: LED; sound: buzzer or speaker; movement: motor

Page 75 Quick Test
1. An electronic component that can be programmed to perform different functions; for example, a microcontroller.
2. Reduce circuit sizes, flexible, support a range of different inputs and outputs
3. Flow chart, block-based editors, raw code

Pages 76–81 Review Questions

Pages 76–81 Material Considerations
1. **a)** The ability to withstand a pulling force [1].
   b) The mass of material per unit volume [1].
   c) The ability of a material to last a long time without being damaged [1].
2. Award marks as indicated, up to a maximum of 6 marks.
   * The visual properties [1], including colour, shape and texture [1], to make it interesting for the baby to look at [1].
   * The tactile properties [1], so it will be comfortable for the baby to hold [1] or feel interesting [1].
   * The sound if it is a rattle [1].
   * The taste of the material [1] as the baby may put it in their mouth [1].
   * Any other relevant pont.
3. Award up to 6 marks as follows (information can be conveyed either by sketches or notes): trees are cut down [1] and turned into pulp [1]. Chemicals are added [1], such as chalk and dye [1], and the paper is formed using a mesh [1]. It is then wound into rolls [1] and subsequently cut to the required size [1].
4. **a)** Award 1 mark each for two suitable applications; for example, mounting of pictures, architectural models.
   b) Award marks as indicated up to a maximum of 4 marks as follows: the core of foam board is polystyrene [1]. This is made from oil [1], a non-renewable resource [1]. It is not biodegradable [1] and cannot be recycled [1], so is normally disposed to landfill or incinerated [1].
5. Award marks as indicated, up to a maximum of 4 marks: hardwoods come from deciduous trees [1] which shed their leaves each autumn [1]. Softwoods come from coniferous trees [1], which keep their leaves all year [1], and which means they typically grow faster than hardwoods [1]. Softwoods also tend to have a more open grain than hardwoods [1].
6. Award up to 4 marks as follows (information can be conveyed either by sketches or notes): trees are cut down [1] and layers of veneer/plies are shaved from them [1]. These are glued together [1] with the grain structure at 90° to each other [1].
7. **a)** A mixture of two or more metals [1].
   b) i) Acceptable answers: stainless steel, mild or low-carbon steel, or cast iron [1].
   ii) 1 mark for any of: (stainless steel) kitchen equipment, medical instruments or any other suitable application; (mild/low-carbon steel) car bodies, table legs or ships; (cast iron) engine blocks, grates or person-hole covers.
   iii) 1 mark each for identifying a requirement of the application and justifying the choice with respect to one of the material properties; for example, tough, strong, hard, difficult to machine, corrosion resistant.
   c) i) Any suitable non-ferrous alloy, for example brass, pewter, solder [1].
   ii) 1 mark for any appropriate application.
   iii) 1 mark each for identifying a requirement of the application and justifying the choice with respect to one of the material properties.
8. Award marks as indicated up to a maximum of 10 marks. Most polymers are made from carbon-based fossil fuels [1] such as oil, gas and coal [1]. These are a finite resource [1] and non-renewable: once they are used they are gone [1]. The extraction

Answers

of these resources and their transportation can also cause damage to the environment [1]. Sustainable polymers are being developed from vegetable products [1], such as corn starch [1]. Synthetic polymers are not normally biodegradable [1]. At the end of their usable life, thermosetting polymers typically end up in landfill [1], which uses up valuable land [1] and can be a cause of pollution [1] and damage to local habitats [1]. Thermoplastics can be recycled [1]. They are normally marked with a symbol to identify their type [1] and they must be sorted before recycling [1]. Any other appropriate response. [1]

9. Natural fibres come from animals or plants [1], whereas synthetic fibres are human-made, usually from oil [1].

10. a) Home use = 12% of 40 million = 0.12 × 40 = £4.8 million [1 mark for method, 1 mark for answer].
    b) Clothing = 15 / 100 = 3 / 20 [1]

11. Award 1 mark each for any two of: levers, linkages, gears, cams, pulleys, belts.

Pages 82–85 Practice Questions

Pages 82–85 Technical Understanding

1. It would weigh less [1], as reinforcement could be applied only where needed [1]; it may also be lower cost [1].
2. 2 × 70° = 140° [1]; 180° − 140° = 40° [1]
3. a) Movement straight in one direction [1]
   b) Movement in a circle [1]
   c) Movement backwards and forwards [1]
   d) Swinging backwards and forwards [1]
4. a) 1 mark for a suitable example; for example, scissors, pliers, seesaw.
   b) Effort = load / mechanical advantage [1] = 24 / 3 = 8 Newtons [1]
5. a) Push–pull linkage [1]
   b) Bevel gears or worm and worm wheel [1]
   c) Cam [1]
   d) Rack and pinion [1]
6. a) Second class [1]
   b) Mechanical advantage = (40 + 80) / 40 = 3 [1 mark for method, 1 mark for correct answer]
7. a) Spur gear [1]
   b) Anticlockwise [1]
   c) Gear ratio = 12 / 36 [1 mark for method] = 1 : 3 [1 mark for answer; must be a ratio: fractions not accepted]
8. a) 1 mark for LDR, light dependent resistor or other suitable named sensor [1]
   b) Light – LED [1] Sound – Buzzer or speaker [1] Movement – Motor [1]
   c) Up to 2 marks for description of function. For example: a tilt switch is used to detect whether something has been moved/tilted [1]. When the switch is tilted the contacts inside are joined by mercury/a small ball bearing. [1]
9. a) 1 mark for microcontroller, PIC or other suitable specific named example [1]
   b) Up to 2 marks for one reason explained. For example: They can be used to add intelligence to products through programming [1], which can be used to enable them to perform a wide range of different functions. [1]; They can support a wide range of input and output devices [1], making them very flexible and suitable for use in a wide range of products. [1]
   c) Up to 2 marks for explanation of one disadvantage. For example: Programmable components can be costly to buy [1] resulting in a more expensive product to produce [1].

Pages 86–103 Revise Questions

Page 87 Quick Test
1. To check how a product will look and function in 3D.
2. Card, polystyrene block, 3 mm MDF, balsa wood
3. To test the effectiveness of a pattern that has been produced for a garment.
4. An onscreen 3D model produced using CAD software.

Page 89 Quick Test
1. Any four of: scalpels, craft knives, compass cutters and circle cutters, rotary trimmers and guillotines
2. Any three of: coping saw, powered fret saw, jigsaw, band saw
3. Pinking shears have a serrated edge.

Page 91 Quick Test
1. Any six from: butt, mitre, lap, halving, housing, dowel, biscuit, mortise and tenon, dovetail
2. Brazing is carried out at a lower temperature and a filler metal with a lower melting point than the parent metal is melted, not the actual metal. It is like soldering, but at very high temperatures. In welding the parent metal parts are fused together.
3. A strip of adhesive web is placed between the two fabrics. Heat from an iron then fuses them together.

Page 93 Quick Test
1. Steam bending and laminating using a former
2. Line bending, press (or yoke) moulding, vacuum forming
3. Make a single or double fold and add stiches at the top or side to hold it in place.

Page 95 Quick Test
1. To ensure that a product is fit for purpose.
2. To ensure that all parts of a product are made the same.
3. The permissible limits of variation in the dimensions or physical properties of a manufactured product or part.
4. Good marking out, good sawing technique, reuse of off-cuts

Page 97 Quick Test
1. Computer-aided design, computer-aided manufacture, computer-aided engineering
2. Easier to modify designs, greater accuracy, designs can be rotated and viewed from different angles.
3. Easier to produce complex shapes, greater accuracy, efficiency and consistency of manufacture.
4. Producing quick prototypes for evaluation.

Page 99 Quick Test
1. For example: chocolate bars, cars, nuts and bolts
2. If suppliers don't deliver on time production will stop, meaning that expensive equipment is standing around unused.
3. Robotics, 3D printing

Page 101 Quick Test
1. Offset lithography, screen process printing, digital printing
2. Furniture industry
3. Metal

Page 103 Quick Test
1. Flat-bed and rotary screen printing
2. 3D printing, stereolithography

Answers

Pages 104–107 Technical Understanding

1. a) 1 mark for each correct response up to 10 marks.

Function	Component	Input or Output
Detect changes in light level	LDR [1]	Input [1]
Produce light	LED [1] or bulb/lamp [1]	Output [1]
Produce sound	Buzzer [1] or speaker [1]	Output [1]
Detect that something has been moved	Tilt switch [1] or infrared sensor [1]	Input [1]
Produce motion	Motor [1]	Output [1]

b) Up to 2 marks for explanation of reason. For example: to protect against environmental changes [1] such as providing weather resistance to rain [1].
2. a) Darts are a type of fold or tuck that come to a point [1]; they are sewn into the fabric [1].
b) Darts provide shape [1], helping to tailor the garment to the wearer [1].
3. Using Pythagoras' theorum, b = √(1000² − 600²) = 800 mm [1 mark for using Pythagoras, 1 mark for inserting the correct values and 1 mark for the correct solution]
4. a) Reciprocating [1]
b) Oscillating [1]
c) Rotary [1]
d) Linear [1]
5. a) Push–pull linkage [1]
b) Rotary [1]
c) Linear [1]
d) Reciprocating [1].
6. Award up to 6 marks as follows. Spur gears would allow greater torque [1], as in a pulley and belt high torque may cause the belt to slip [1]. The pulley and belt may weigh less than the gears [1] as the gears would have to be large enough to mesh/touch [1] whereas the pulleys could be small and only connected by the belt [1]. The belt on the pulley system could stretch to absorb shocks [1], which could otherwise damage the gears [1]. The pulley and belt may be easier to manufacture than the gears [1], which could mean that it costs less [1]. Any other appropriate response.
7. a) 1 mark for each appropriate input and output, such as LDR (input) and LED (output).
b) Up to 2 marks for each reason explained. For example: A single programmable component could replace a whole timing circuit [1], leading to a smaller product [1]. Programmable components can be reprogrammed [1], so the time period of the light could be shortened if the child gets less scared of the dark [1].

Pages 108–113 Manufacturing Processes and Techniques

1. a) Up to 2 marks for each definition. For example:
   - Toile: early version of a garment [1] made from cheap material [1].
   - Iterative design: an approach where a design is incrementally developed/refined [1] based on testing/feedback [1].
b) 1 mark for each suitable material. For example: card [1], foam board [1], thin MDF [1].
2. a) Award 1 mark each for any two of: rotary cutter, scissors, pinking shears.
b) Award marks as follows:
   - It allows a garment to increase fullness or widen out, modifying the shape [1].
   - It allows a longer piece of fabric to be attached within the length of a shorter piece [1].
3. a) Award 1 mark for housing joint.
b) Award 1 mark for halving joint.
c) Award 1 mark for mortise and tenon.
d) Award 1 mark for dowel joint.
e) Award 1 mark for dovetail joint.
4. 9–12 marks: thorough knowledge and understanding of how accuracy can be ensured when manufacturing products. All points fully explained. Several relevant examples presented to support answer. 5–8 marks: good knowledge and understanding of how accuracy can be ensured when manufacturing products. Majority of points explained. Some relevant examples presented to support answer. 1–4 marks: limited knowledge or understanding. Mainly descriptive response. Few or no relevant examples presented to support answer.

   Indicative answer: Accurate measuring and marking out results in parts/products that are cut more accurately. Tools such as jigs, templates and patterns can be used to ensure accuracy. For example, a jig can be set up to hold and guide a drill, thus ensuring holes are drilled in the same place on each piece of material. A template can be drawn round to ensure a part is produced exactly the same each time it is cut. Tolerances are shown on drawings and/or specifications. They should be followed to ensure the product/part is produced within these permissible limits of variation.
5. 1 mark for each suitable advantage and disadvantage. For example:
   - Advantages: increased accuracy of design [1], easier to make changes to design [1], complex designs can be created quickly [1].
   - Disadvantages: initial cost of software can be high [1], requires access to suitable ICT hardware [1].
6. Award up to 10 marks as follows. One-off/bespoke production leads to the highest cost per product [1] as it requires the most labour time per product [1] and this labour is provided by highly skilled craftsmen [1]. Batch production groups identical products together which means that there is less non-making time due to equipment changeovers [1]. Dedicated jigs may be used to speed up production on some processes [1]. Some processes may be automated, speeding up production [1], as the cost can be divided between the quantity of products made [1]. Mass production leads to the lowest cost per product [1] when large quantities of products are made [1]. Tools and equipment are dedicated to making one product [1], which means no time is lost to changing between products [1]. Jigs and fixtures will be used to speed up production [1]. Most processes will be automated, also speeding up production [1]. Labour costs are

Answers

typically lower [1], as some lower-skill workers are used for production line roles [1]. Any other relevant point. [1]

7. Award marks as follows. Metal blades are positioned in the shape to be cut [1]. These are pushed into the card [1]. Foam rubber around the blade compresses during cutting and pushes to release the cut material [1].

8. Award 1 mark each for: to make grooves [1] and edge profiles [1].

9. To provide a professional finish to seams and hems/to provide a decorative finish [1].

10. Award marks as follows. It is used to apply patterns or images to long lengths of fabric [1]. Ink is applied to a series of different rollers in contact with the fabric [1]. Each roller has a pattern/image and normally applies a different colour [1]. The fabric moves continuously [1].

Pages 114–119 Review Questions

Pages 114–119 Manufacturing Processes and Techniques

1. a) Up to 2 marks for explanation of each reason. For example: shows how the product will look in 3D [1] so that stakeholders can decide whether they are happy or not with the design [1]. Potential problems with the design can be identified early [1] thus avoiding waste of more expensive materials/components [1].
    b) Up to 2 marks for explanation of each reason. For example: card is easy to cut to size/shape [1] so specialist cutting tools are not needed [1]. It is cheap to buy [1] so can be used in large quantities [1].

2. a) Award 1 mark for epoxy resin.
    b) Award 1 mark for polyvinyl acetate (PVA).
    c) Award 1 mark for solvent cement.

3. Award marks as follows (information can be conveyed either by sketches or notes). A thermoplastic sheet is heated in an oven until it is flexible [1]. It is then pressed between two moulds [1]. The moulds are male and female/mould and yoke [1]. It is allowed to cool and hardens into the shape of the mould [1].

4. Award 1 mark each for any two of: heat/using a laser cutter, machining processes/milling/routing, using corrosive chemicals.

5. a) Up to 2 marks for each definition. For example:
    * Jig: a custom tool [1] for making sure parts of a product are exactly the same [1].
    * Tolerance: the permissible limits of variation [1] in the dimensions of a manufactured product [1].
    b) Up to 3 marks for explanation. For example: failure to use tolerances could result in improper fits [1], which would result in the product being rejected by clients/stakeholders [1]. This would add extra cost and time as the product would need to be remade [1].

6. 1 mark for each suitable advantage and disadvantage. For example: Advantages: consistency of production [1], high levels of manufacturing accuracy [1], high speed of manufacture [1]. Disadvantages: initial cost of machinery can be high [1], time/cost of training staff to use machinery [1].

7. Award 1 mark for each suitable example given. one-off: tailored suit, satellites; batch: furniture, clothes for high street stores; mass: chocolate bars, bottles, cars.

8. Award up to a maximum of 4 marks as follows. A reusable metal mould is made. [1] Molten metal is poured into a cylinder/into the die casting machine. [1] A ram then forces this metal into the mould. [1] Pressure is held until the metal solidifies and cools. [1] The mould is then opened and the component removed [1].

9. a) Suppliers deliver materials only when they are needed/about to be used. [1]
    b) Award up to 2 marks each for a suitable advantage and disadvantage. For example:

Advantage: the company has less stock [1], meaning less money is tied up in materials [1] and that less space is required for storage [1].
Disadvantage: if suppliers fail to deliver on time or there are quality problems [1], this can stop production [1] meaning that expensive equipment is standing around unused.

10. Award marks as follows (information can be conveyed either by sketches or notes). A split mould is made in the shape of the bottle [1]. Air is blown into an extruded section of plastic tube [1]. The air forces plastic to the sides of the mould [1]. The mould is then cooled and the product is removed [1].

Pages 120–129 Mix it Up Questions

Pages 120–129 Mixed Exam-Style Questions

1. 1 mark for showing how/where the program starts and ends, 1 mark for way of checking the switch has been pressed, 1 mark for turning on the buzzer after the switch has been pressed, 1 mark for way of setting the correct time period, 1 mark for turning the buzzer off, 1 mark for turning on the LED. Any appropriate programming language may be used, including raw code, block- or flow-chart-based approaches.

2. a) Up to 3 marks for description of the process. For example: fossil fuels are burned to create steam [1]. The steam turns turbines [1] which drive generators to produce electricity [1].
    b) 1 mark for non-renewable.
    c) Up to 2 marks for explanation of advantage and 2 marks for explanation of disadvantage. For example:
    Advantage: reduces reliance on fossil fuels for generating energy [1], which results in less greenhouse gases being released into the atmosphere [1].
    Disadvantage: accidents can result in radiation being released into the atmosphere [1]. This can lead to serious health problems for people living nearby [1].

3. 9–12 marks: thorough knowledge and understanding of the reasons why designers explore existing products. All points fully explained. Several relevant examples presented to support answer. 5–8 marks: good knowledge and understanding of the reasons why designers explore existing products. Majority of points explained. Some relevant examples presented to support answer. 1–4 marks: limited knowledge or understanding. Mainly descriptive response. Few or no relevant examples presented to support answer.

Indicative answer: Exploring existing products allows designers to learn from the successes and failures of the past. It gives them inspiration and ideas for new products. Existing designs can be developed to produce improved and better products. Designers can learn about materials, processes and components used in products. This helps them to build their own working knowledge of these. Designers can learn about how products have been affected by trends/fashion and apply this to produce designs that meet with current popular trends. Designers can learn about the positive or negative effects that products have had on the environment. This can help them to design more sustainable products in the future. For example, learning about the use of renewable energy sources can lead to products that have less carbon emissions, such as solar-powered lighting.

4. a) Up to 2 marks for definition. For example:
    Basic: computer-aided design [1].
    Detailed: the use of computer software to produce designs for products [2].
    b) Up to 2 marks for definition. For example:
    Basic: computer-aided manufacture [1].
    Detailed: the use of computer software to control machine tools to manufacture products [2].

c) Up to 2 marks for definition. For example:
Basic: computer-aided engineering **[1]**.
Detailed: the use of computer software to aid in engineering analysis tasks **[2]**.

5. a) 1 mark for statement. For example: a drawing follows formal conventions whereas a sketch does not **[1]**.
   b) Up to 2 marks for definition. For example: shows the parts of a product separated **[1]** and the relationship between them **[1]**.
   c) 1 mark for suitable example for each type of communication. For example:
   Flow chart: producing an order of operations for manufacture **[1]**.
   Mathematical modelling: analysing the effectiveness of a batch manufacturing process **[1]**.

6. a) Award marks as follows up to a maximum of 5 marks (information can be in either sketches or notes). Plastic powder or granules are fed from a hopper into the machine **[1]**. Heaters melt the plastic **[1]**. A screw moves the plastic along towards the mould **[1]**. The screw provides pressure on the plastic, forcing it into the mould **[1]**. Pressure is maintained on the mould until it has cooled enough to be opened **[1]**.
   b) Material needed = $20\,000 \times 2.4 \times 10^{-5} = 0.48$ m^3 **[1]**; material lost = $0.5 - 0.48 = 0.02$ m^3 or 20×10^{-3} m^3 **[1]**
   c) Profit = $8.00 - 6.40 = £1.60$ **[1]**; % profit = $1.60 / 8.00 \times 100/1 = 20\%$ **[1]**

7. Award marks as follows. A hole is drilled in two metal sheets **[1]**. The rivet is pushed through the hole **[1]**. The blank end is hammered to form a second head **[1]**.

8. Award marks as follows up to a maximum of 10 marks (information can be in either sketches or notes). A pattern is made, normally in wood **[1]**. This is sandwiched between two boxes of oiled sand **[1]**. The boxes are called the cope and the drag **[1]**. The sand is compressed around the pattern **[1]**. The cope and drag are carefully separated and the pattern removed, leaving a hollow shape when they are reassembled **[1]**. There will be a hole for a runner, to allow the metal to be poured in **[1]**. There will also be a hole for a riser, to let air escape **[1]**. The metal is melted **[1]**. Metal is poured in through the runner **[1]**. Once the metal has cooled, the sand mould can be broken/shaken off **[1]**. The runner and riser can be cut off **[1]**. Any excess metal/flash will be removed and the casting trimmed or cleaned by fettling **[1]**.

9. a) Bevel gear or worm and worm gear **[1]**
   b) Push–pull linkage **[1]**
   c) Cam **[1]**
   d) 'Moving wings' linkage **[1]**
   e) Rack and pinion **[1]**

10. The ability of a material to be deformed, shaped and moulded **[1]**.

11. a) Award up to 6 marks as follows: the sheet would need to be marked out **[1]**, then cut using a rotary trimmer or guillotine **[1]**. The perforations for the tear-off tags **[1]** could be made using a perforation cutter **[1]**. The fold could be either manually scored **[1]**, e.g. using scissors **[1]**, then folded, or creased **[1]** with a creasing bar **[1]** then folded.
    b) Die cutting **[1]**.

12. Award marks as follows. 7–9 marks: thorough knowledge and understanding of the properties required, with a minimum of five properties considered. Explanations are given of why all the identified properties are needed. 4–6 marks: good knowledge and understanding of the properties required, with a minimum of three properties considered. Explanation included for why some of the identified properties are needed. 1–3 marks: limited knowledge or understanding. Mainly descriptive response, stating a few of the properties required.
Properties specific to the application that could be considered include:

Food packaging	Ability to prevent spoilage of contents or damage to the packaging Ability to be printed, to give aesthetic appeal Cost
Flat-pack furniture	Toughness, to resist impacts Hardness, to resist being scratched or damaged in use Cost
Electrical system in a fridge	Absorbency and resistance to corrosion, so that it isn't damaged by the materials, water or food that contact it in use Strength, to support whatever is put into it and to resist damage if someone sits on it! Electrical conductivity – it should insulate the circuitry to prevent electric shocks to the user
Plastic socket for an electric plug	Electrical conductivity: it should be an insulator to protect the user from the electrical circuit inside it Toughness, so that it doesn't break if accidentally knocked, causing safety issues
Fabric covering for a sofa	Aesthetics – colour and texture that appeal to the user Hardwearing so it lasts a long time Non-flammable, so that it doesn't burn
Metal hammer	Strength Toughness, to resist impact if hit or dropped Malleability, ability to be made into the shape of the tool (as material is very hard and may be difficult to form)

In addition, general properties considered (in addition to the above list, where not duplicated) could include: functionality, aesthetics, environmental considerations, availability of materials, cost, social factors, ethical considerations and cultural factors.

Glossary

Absorbency the ability of a material to draw in moisture, light or heat

Accuracy the degree of closeness of a measurement to its true value

Adhesive a chemical used to stick or glue objects together

Aesthetics how an object appeals to the five senses

Alloy a mixture of two or more metals

Annotation adding labels identifying and explaining the key features on a drawing

Anthropometric data measurements that are taken from millions of people of different shapes and sizes and placed in charts

Batch production making a series of groups of identical products

Bill of materials a list of the materials and/or components needed to manufacture an end product

Biodegradable material a material that decomposes rapidly as a result of the action of microorganisms

Biodegrade decompose or rot due to interaction with the environment

Bioplastics plastics made using biological substances instead of oil

Biopolymer a polymeric substance produced by living organisms

Bleaching a finish for fabrics that removes all natural colour

Blow moulding a process used to shape hollow polymer products

Bonding a method of joining fabrics without stitching

Boning using rigid strips of material to maintain the shape of a textile product

Brazing a joining process for metals where a filler metal is melted to join parts together at high temperature

CAD computer-aided design

Cam a mechanism that converts rotary motion to reciprocating motion

Casting pouring molten metal into a mould to form a product

Circular economy a model that aims to increase the use of renewable energy and design products that are 'made to be made again'

CNC computer numerical control, using a string of numbers to control the movements of a machine

Commercial impact how well a product sells and generates revenue

Composite a material made up of two or more other materials that are not chemically combined

Compression moulding a process used to shape products from thermosetting polymer

Computer-aided design (CAD) the use of computer software to produce designs for products

Computer-aided engineering (CAE) the use of computer software to aid in engineering analysis tasks

Computer-aided manufacture (CAM) the use of computer software to control machine tools to manufacture products

Concept model a model produced to illustrate the overall concept of a proposed product

Corrosion resistance the ability of a material not to be damaged by its environment

Crating a drawing technique that uses boxes to act as a guideline for drawings

Darts folds coming to a point that are sewn into fabric to provide shape

Density mass of material per unit volume

Design brief a short description of a design problem and how it is to be solved

Design classic a product that has had a large influence on the world of design or the wider public

Die casting a process where molten metal is shaped using pressure and a reusable mould

Die cutting a process that uses metal blades and a press to cut a shape in paper or card

Disruptive technology an innovation that creates a new market or way of doing things

Driver circuit a circuit that is used to boost current levels to those needed by an output device

Durability the ability of a material to last a long time without being damaged

Economies of scale a saving in cost per product gained by making a higher number of products

Effort the force applied to something (for example to a lever)

Elasticity the ability of a material to return to its original shape when a force on it is removed

Electrical conductivity the ability of electricity to pass through a material

Electronic system a collection of input, process, driver and output stages that respond to, change and produce different types of signal

End user the person or people that will use a product when it is completed

Ergonomics the study of how people interact with the products and systems around them

Etching the use of a chemical, heat or machine to remove selected parts of a material surface

Ethical design designing with regard to people's principles, beliefs and morals

Exclusive design design of products for a limited audience

Exploded drawing a picture that shows how the parts of a product fit together

Exploring existing designs analysing and critiquing designs that have already been produced

Extrusion making a sectional shape by pushing material through a die

Fair trade a movement that works to help people in developing countries get a fair deal for the products that they produce

Ferrous metal metal that contains a significant amount of iron

Finite resource a resource of which there is only a limited quantity

Flammability how easily a material burns

Flow chart a diagram that shows the order in which a series of commands or events is carried out

Fossil fuel fuel created from the remains of dead organisms over a long period of time; for example, coal, oil and gas

Fulcrum   the pivot point of a lever
Function   how a product or system works and/or what it does
Functionality   how well a product fulfils the purpose it needs to meet

Gathering   a sewing technique that allows a garment to increase fullness or widen out, or for shortening the length of a strip of fabric; allows a longer piece to be attached to a shorter piece
Gear   a mechanism used to transfer rotary motion, which can also change the direction or magnitude of the force transmitted
Grain   the growth rings visible on the surface of the wood
Graphene   a form of carbon consisting of sheets which are one atom thick
gsm   grams per square metre; the thickness of paper or card

Hardness   the resistance of a material to wear and abrasion
Hardwood   wood from deciduous trees that shed their leaves each autumn
Hydro energy   energy that is taken from flowing water, typically by releasing water from a dam to turn turbines

Inclusive design   design of products that can be used by everyone without special adaptations
Injection moulding   a process used to shape polymer products
Input device   a device that turns a real-world signal, such as light, sound or movement, into an electronic signal
Integrated circuit (IC)   a complete electronic circuit contained on a single small microchip
Isometric projection   a scaled 3D drawing with sides at an angle of 30° to the baseline
Iterative design   a cyclic design approach where each iteration is tested, evaluated and refined, resulting in a new iteration

Jig   a custom-made tool designed to achieve accuracy, repeatability and interchangeability during product manufacture
Just-in-time manufacturing   manufacturing where items from suppliers are delivered only when they are needed

Knitted   made from yarn using interlocking loops

Laminating (paper and card)   a finishing technique for paper and cardboard that is created by applying a plastic film to one or both sides of the material
Laminating (other material)   overlaying a flat object or sheet of material with a layer of protective material
Layering   adding multiple layers of material to a textile product to increase its strength
Lean manufacturing   a systematic approach to eliminate all forms of waste in manufacturing
Lever   a simple device that pivots about a fulcrum
Life cycle assessment   a tool for systematically evaluating the environmental aspects of a product or system
Line bending   a process that involves bending thermoplastic along a heated line

Linear   moving in a straight line
Linkage   an assembly of parts used to transfer motion between two mechanisms, which can also change the direction or magnitude of the force transmitted

Malleable   pliable, able to be pressed or forced into shape without breaking
Marketing   the act of promoting or advertising a product or system
Mass production   making the same product on a large scale
Mathematical model   a representation of a product or system using mathematical formulae
Microcontroller   a small computer on a chip that is designed for use in control applications
Model   a 3D representation of a proposed product, often scaled down
Moulding   using a former to shape a material

Nanomaterial   a material made up of particles that are less than 100 nm (nanometres) in size
Nanotechnology   functional systems developed at the molecular or 'nano' scale
Natural fibres   fibres from sources such as animals and plants
New and emerging technologies   technologies that are new, currently being developed or that will be developed in the next 5–10 years
Non-ferrous metal   metal that does not contain iron
Non-renewable energy source   an energy source that cannot replenish itself quickly and therefore will eventually run out
Nuclear energy   energy that is created by making use of highly controlled nuclear reactions, such as nuclear fission

Offset lithography   a printing process for paper and board
One-off/bespoke production   making a single product to a customer specification
Oscillating   swinging in alternate directions
Output device   a device that turns an electronic signal into a real-world signal, such as light, sound or movement
Overlocker   a specialised sewing machine used for joining fabrics
Pattern   a type of template that is used to trace the shape of parts of a garment onto fabric before it is cut
Perforation   a hole in a material
Plasticity   the ability of a material to be shaped or moulded
Pleating   making a double or multiple fold in a textile product, held by stitching
Polishing   a finishing technique used to protect and improve the aesthetics of metals and plastics
Polymer   a material made from chains of a repeating chemical part called a monomer
Pressing   applying pressure to deform a material
Process   changes an electronic signal to create functions such as timing, latching and counting
Pulley   a mechanism comprising two wheels linked by a belt; this transfers rotary motion and can also change the direction or magnitude of the force transmitted
Punching   a wasting process that forces a tool through a material to create a hole

Glossary

Rapid prototyping   an additive manufacturing technology used to produce a 3D product in a single operation from a CAD model

Reciprocating   moving backwards and forwards

Recycle   to reprocess or convert waste back into a useful material

Reinforcing   adding strength or stiffness to a product

Rendering   applying colour, shade and texture to a drawing to make it look more realistic

Renewable energy source   a source that can replenish itself quickly and therefore will not run out

Rotating   turning in a circle

Rotational moulding   a process used to shape polymer products

Scale   the ratio of the size of a drawn object to the size of the object

Self-finishing material   a material that is already manufactured with a good surface finish

Selvedge   an edge of a fabric that won't fray

Sewing   a method of joining fabrics by stitching with thread

Shearing   a wasting process used to cut material

Sketch modelling   creating a 3D object from a 2D shape using CAD software

Smart materials   materials whose properties change as a result of external stimuli, such as heat or light or pressure

Softwood   wood from trees that maintain their foliage all year round

Solar energy   energy that is taken from the sun, typically by using solar panels to harness sunlight and convert it into electricity

Soldering   a joining process for metals where a filler metal is melted to join parts together

Stakeholder   a person with a business interest in a product being designed and developed

Standard components   common parts that are commercially available in specified sizes

Stiffness   how rigid an object is

Stock form   the shape of material commonly available from a supplier

Strength   the ability of a material to withstand a force that is applied to it

Superalloy   a metal alloy that can withstand exceptional temperatures, stresses or corrosive environments

Sustainable   naturally replenished within a short period of time

Sustainable development   development that meets the needs of the present without compromising the ability of future generations to meet their needs

Synthetic   made by people; not natural

Synthetic fibres   human-made fibres; typically from fossil fuels

Systems-based approach   a top-down design approach that starts with an overview of the overall system in terms of its input, process and output sub-systems

Technical textile   fabric made for its performance properties rather than aesthetic characteristics

Template   used to draw a shape onto material which can then be cut around

Thermal conductivity   the ability of heat to pass through a material

Thermoplastic polymer   a polymer that can be reshaped when it is heated

Thermosetting polymer   a polymer that will not change its shape when heated

Toile   an early version of a piece of clothing, usually made from cheap materials

Tolerance   the permissible limits of variation in the dimensions or physical properties of a manufactured product or part

Toughness   the ability of a material to absorb an impact without rupturing

Triangulation   dividing a structure into triangles to reinforce it

Turning   using a lathe to create a product with a round profile by wasting

User-centred design   a design approach where the needs and wants of the end user are considered extensively at each stage of the design process

Vacuum forming   a process where heated plastic is formed onto a mould using a vacuum

Varnishing   a finishing technique for timber where varnish is applied to protect the wood underneath

Veneer   a thin layer of wood

Viability   when a product is not only purchased initially, but performs well enough for it to be recommended to others, and for sales to continue

Wasting   removal of material

Welding   a joining process for metals where the parts are melted along the joint line by heat

Wind energy   energy that is taken from the wind, typically by using wind turbines to generate electricity

Woven   made from interlaced threads

Yarn   spun and twisted thread made from fibres

Notes

Notes

Index

Index

Collins

OCR GCSE 9-1

Design and Technology

Workbook

OCR
GCSE 9-1

Workbook

Paul Anderson and David Hills-Taylor

Contents

Design Considerations

Communicating Design Ideas

Material Considerations

Technical Understanding

Manufacturing Processes and Techniques

Exploring Context and Factors Affecting the Design Process

1 Designers must consider several factors when exploring the design context.

Give **seven** different considerations that designers should think about when exploring the design context.

1 ....

2 ....

3 ....

4 ....

5 ....

6 ....

7 ....   [7]

2 Explain **two** reasons why designers meet with clients to discuss the design context.

1 ....

....

....

....

....   [2]

2 ....

....

....

....

....   [2]

Total Marks .... / 11

Usability

1 Discuss the importance of using anthropometric data when designing products.
Use examples to support your answer.

_____

_____

_____

_____

_____

_____

_____

_____

_____

_____

_____

_____

_____

_____

_____

_____

_____

_____

_____ [9]

Total Marks .... / 9

Exploring Existing Designs

1 Designers must consider several factors when exploring existing designs.

Give **seven** different considerations that designers should think about when exploring existing designs.

1 ....

....

2 ....

....

3 ....

....

4 ....

....

5 ....

....

6 ....

....

7 ....

....

....

[7]

2 State what is meant by life cycle assessment.

....

....

....

[1]

Total Marks .... / 8

New and Emerging Technologies

1 Give **one** example of a new and emerging technology that could have a positive impact on sustainability. Explain how it could do this.

New and emerging technology

Explanation

[3]

2 Give **one** example of a new and emerging technology that could have a positive impact on people's lifestyles. Explain how it could do this.

New and emerging technology

Explanation

[3]

Total Marks .... / 6

Sources of Energy

1 The table shows different sources of energy.

Complete the table by stating whether each is renewable or non-renewable and describing how each is used to produce energy.

Source of Energy	Renewable or Non-Renewable	Description of How Energy is Produced
Nuclear fuel		
Solar energy		
Wind energy		

[9]

Total Marks _____ / 9

Wider Influences on Designing and Making

1 Explain **three** ways that a product can be designed to be more sustainable.

1 ....

....

....

....

2 ....

....

....

....

3 ....

....

....

.... [6]

2 What is meant by the term 'fair trade'?

....

....

....

....

....

.... [2]

3 State what is meant by ethical design.

....

.... [1]

Total Marks .... / 9

Viability of Design Solutions

1 What is meant by the viability of a product or system?

[2]

2 Discuss the factors that affect the commercial viability of a product.

[6]

Total Marks .... / 8

Graphical Techniques 1

1. Produce a 3D sketch of a table suitable for use in a school classroom.

   Annotate your sketch to show the materials and manufacturing processes that would be used to make the table. Explain why you have chosen them.

[5]

Total Marks .... / 5

Graphical Techniques 2

1 **a)** State the purpose of a flow chart.

....

.... [1]

b) Explain **two** benefits of using a flow chart to plan the steps needed to manufacture a product.

1 ....

....

....

....

....

2 ....

....

....

....

.... [4]

2 Explain **two** reasons why a designer would create an exploded drawing of a design for a product.

1 ....

....

....

....

2 ....

....

....

.... [4]

> **Total Marks** .... / 9

Approaches to Designing

1 The table shows three of the main approaches to designing.

Complete the table by giving **one** advantage and **one** disadvantage of each design approach.

Design Approach	Advantage of Approach	Disadvantage of Approach
Iterative design		
User-centred design		
Systems thinking		

[6]

Properties of Materials

1 State the meaning of the following properties.

a) Toughness

_____

_____

_____ [1]

b) Electrical conductivity

_____

_____

_____ [1]

c) Elasticity

_____

_____

_____ [1]

2 Name the material property described by each of the following statements.

a) The ability of a material to resist being damaged by its environment

_____ [1]

b) How strong the material is divided by its density

_____ [1]

c) The ability of a material to draw in moisture, light or heat

_____ [1]

3 Explain the difference between a physical property and a mechanical property of a material.

_____

_____

_____

_____

_____ [2]

Total Marks _____ / 8

Factors Influencing Material Selection

1 Explain what is meant by the following terms.

a) Functionality

....

.... [1]

b) Aesthetics

....

.... [1]

2 A designer has been asked to review the choice of materials for a product, to make it more environmentally friendly.

Explain the **environmental factors** the designer may consider when recommending an alternative material.

....

....

....

....

....

....

....

....

....

....

....

....

....

.... [6]

Total Marks .... / 8

Paper and Board

1 Explain the differences between carton board and bleached card.

....

....

....

....

....

....

....

.... [4]

2 A manufacturer has to cut as many copies as possible of the following shape from a piece of foam board.

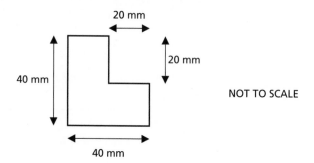

NOT TO SCALE

Sketching on the representation of the board provided, show how you would lay out the shapes to minimise waste.

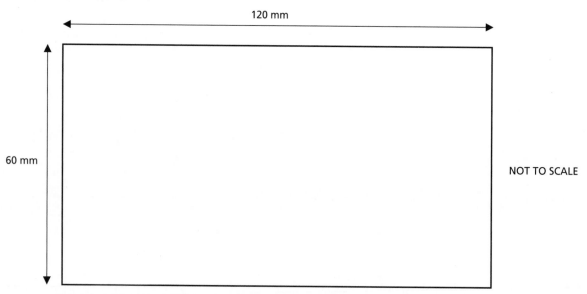

NOT TO SCALE

[2]

Total Marks .... / 6

Timber

1. Using notes and sketches, explain how the differences between plywood and blockboard affect their properties.

[4]

2. Compare the **environmental impact** of using solid oak with that of using MDF to make furniture products.

[6]

Total Marks _____ / 10

Metals

1 Name the metallic elements that are the major components of the following metal alloys.

a) Stainless steel

....

.... [2]

b) Solder

....

.... [2]

c) Pewter

....

.... [2]

d) Brass

....

.... [2]

2 a) Name **four** stock forms in which metal is commonly available.

1 ....

2 ....

3 ....

4 .... [4]

b) Explain why a designer may modify a design so that a manufacturer can use metal in stock form.

....

....

....

....

....

.... [4]

Total Marks .... / 16

Polymers

1 Using notes and/or sketches, describe how thermoplastic polymers are produced from their raw materials.

[4]

2 A manufacturer is producing solid plastic cubes. Each cube is 30 mm on each side. The manufacturer is using a polymer with a density of 960 kg m^{-3}.

Calculate the mass of material needed to make 10 000 cubes. Assume that no material is wasted during the process.

[5]

Total Marks .... / 9

Textiles

1 a) Name a natural fibre that is used to make fabric.

.... [1]

b) Give a typical use for this fabric.

.... [1]

c) Explain why this fibre is an appropriate choice for this application.

....

....

....

....

.... [3]

2 a) Name a synthetic fibre that is used to make fabric.

....

.... [1]

b) Give a typical use for this fabric.

....

.... [1]

c) Explain why this fibre is an appropriate choice for this application.

....

....

....

....

.... [3]

Total Marks _____ / 10

New Developments in Materials

1 Name a composite material and a typical application for which it is used.

a) Material

.... [1]

b) Application

....

.... [1]

2 Explain why superalloys are used in advanced aircraft engines.

....

....

....

....

....

.... [3]

3 A company manufactures disposable knives and forks from polymers.

Explain why they may prefer to use a biopolymer rather than a synthetic polymer.

....

....

....

....

....

....

....

.... [4]

Total Marks .... / 9

Standard Components

1 Name **two** standard components that are used with each of the following materials.

a) Paper

1 ....

2 .... [2]

b) Fabric

1 ....

2 .... [2]

c) Metal

1 ....

2 .... [2]

d) Timber

1 ....

2 .... [2]

2 Explain why a company may decide to use standard components in a product.

....

....

....

....

....

....

....

.... [4]

Total Marks .... / 12

Finishing Materials

1 The table shows different types of material.

Complete the table by giving **two** finishing techniques that are suitable for use with each type of material.

Type of Material	Finishing Technique 1	Finishing Technique 2
Paper and board		
Timber		
Metal		
Polymer/plastic		
Fibres and fabrics		

[10]

Total Marks _____ / 10

Structural Integrity

1 A manufacturer is designing a casing for a hand-held torch similar to the one shown.

During testing they have found that the casing was bending out of shape when it was held by the user.

Explain how they could reduce the risk of the casing deforming.

....

....

....

....

.... **[4]**

2 Interfacing is a technique used in textiles.

a) Explain the purpose of interfacing.

....

....

....

....

.... **[2]**

b) Give an example of a textile product where interfacing in commonly used.

....

.... **[1]**

Total Marks .... / 7

Motion and Levers

1   State which type of motion is represented by each of the following descriptions.

a) Swinging backwards and forwards

.... [1]

b) Moving straight in one direction

.... [1]

c) Moving in a circle

.... [1]

d) Moving backwards and forwards

.... [1]

2   A first-class lever is being used to raise a load of 60 N. The effort needed to move the load is 24 N.

Calculate how far the load was applied from the fulcrum (length A).

....

....

....

....

....

.... [4]

Total Marks .... / 8

Mechanical Devices

1 Using notes and/or sketches, describe how the design of a cam can change the motion output from the follower in contact with it.

[4]

2 Two bevel gears similar to those shown are being used in a mechanical device.

The input gear has 48 teeth and rotates at a rate of 60 revolutions per minute (rpm).

If the output gear needs to rotate at a rate of 240 rpm, how many teeth does it need to have?

Not to scale

[4]

Total Marks _____ / 8

Electronic Systems

1. The table shows different electronic components.

Complete the table by stating whether each component is an input or output device and giving an example application of each in a product.

Component	Input or Output	Application
Push switch		
Light-emitting diode (LED)		
Motor		
Light-dependent resistor (LDR)		
Buzzer		

[10]

Total Marks .... / 10

Programmable Components

1 A design is being produced for an outdoor security light system. A programmable component is to be used to control how the system works.

The programmable system must:

- Respond to a sensor detecting movement
- Turn on the light for a period of 10 seconds after the sensor has detected movement
- Turn off the light after the time period has ended.

Write a program that meets the needs of the security light system described above. You may use any programming language that you are familiar with.

[5]

Total Marks _____ / 5

Modelling Processes

1 Choose **one** modelling technique that you have studied.

Use notes and sketches to describe how you would produce a 3D model of a design using this technique.

Include details of all tools and equipment that you would use.

Modelling technique chosen:

[6]

Total Marks _____ / 6

Wastage

1 The table lists the tools and equipment used for wasting different materials.

Complete the missing information. The first row has been completed as an example.

Material	Tool	Used for
Paper	Punch	Making holes
Wood	a) .... [1]	Making straight cuts by hand
Thin card	Compass cutters	b) .... [1]
c) .... [1]	Tin snips	Cutting thin sheet
d) .... [1]	Rotary trimmer	e) .... [1]
Textiles	f) .... [1]	Cutting a serrated edge to stop material fraying
Metal	g) .... [1]	Turning round parts

Total Marks .... / 7

Additive Manufacturing Processes

1 Describe the process of joining two metal parts using welding.

[6]

2 Explain how brazing is different to welding.

[4]

3 Name a metal joining technique that does not use heat.

[1]

Total Marks _____ / 11

Deforming and Reforming

1 Using notes and/or sketches, describe how a product is made using vacuum forming.

[10]

Ensuring Accuracy

1 Explain **one** reason why accuracy of manufacture is important.

[2]

2 Explain **one** example of how **each** of the following tools can be used to ensure accuracy of manufacture of a product or part.

Jig

Pattern

[4]

Total Marks .... / 6

Digital Design Tools

1. Give **two** examples of where a designer could use image creation and manipulation software as part of the design process.

   1 ....

   ....

   2 ....

   .... [2]

2. Define the term 'digital manufacture'.

   ....

   ....

   .... [1]

3. Define the term 'rapid prototyping'.

   ....

   ....

   .... [1]

4. Explain **one** benefit of rapid prototyping products.

   ....

   ....

   ....

   ....

   .... [2]

Total Marks .... / 6

Scales of Manufacture

1 a) State what is meant by batch manufacturing.

....

....

....

.... [2]

b) Give **two** examples of products that are made by batch manufacturing:

1 ....

2 .... [2]

2 Explain how moving to lean manufacturing can reduce costs in a manufacturing company.

....

....

....

....

....

....

....

....

.... [8]

Total Marks .... / 12

Large-Scale Processes: Paper, Timber and Metals

1 Using notes and/or sketches, describe how the process of offset lithography is carried out.

[5]

2 A manufacturer has an order from a customer for 10 identical cast parts.

Explain why the manufacturer might prefer to use sand casting rather than die casting for this task.

[4]

Total Marks _____ / 9

Large-Scale Processes: Polymers and Fabrics

1 Discuss the advantages and disadvantages of making a prototype of a product using a rapid prototyping process rather than by conventional machining processes.

[4]

2 Using notes and/or sketches, describe how extruded tubes are made from polymer.

[5]

Collins

GCSE Design & Technology

GCSE (9–1) Design and Technology

Principles of Design and Technology

Question Paper　　　　　　　　　　　Time allowed: 2 hours

You must have:

- the Insert.

You may use:

- a scientific calculator
- a ruler
- geometrical instruments.

Instructions

- Use black ink. Pencil may be used for diagrams and graphs only.
- Answer **all** the questions.
- The Insert will be found on pages 201–208. It must be used when answering the questions in **Section B**.
- Where appropriate, your answers should be supported with working. Marks may be given for a correct method even if the answer is incorrect.
- Write your answer to each question in the space provided. Additional paper may be used if necessary.

Information

- The total mark for this paper is **100**.
- The marks for each question are shown in brackets [ ].
- Quality of extended responses will be assessed in questions marked with an asterisk (*).

Name: _____

Section A

1   A pair of running shoes is shown in Fig. 1.

Fig. 1

(a) Explain **three** factors that should be considered when evaluating the design of the running shoes.

1 ....

....

....

.... [2]

2 ....

....

....

.... [2]

3 ....

....

....

.... [2]

(b) The running shoes are to be sold directly to consumers at a cost of £40. The cost of making one pair of running shoes is £25.

Calculate the percentage profit that will be made.

[2]

(c) Sketches of first ideas were produced during product design.

Explain **two** reasons why a designer would create 2D or 3D sketches of their initial ideas for a product.

1

[2]

2

[2]

(d) Explain **two** benefits of using sketch modelling as part of the design process.

1 ....

....

....

.... [2]

2 ....

....

....

.... [2]

2   A manufacturing company is planning to make a games controller similar to that shown in Fig. 2.

Fig. 2

(a) The casing of the controller will be made from a thermoplastic polymer.

  (i) Name a suitable thermoplastic polymer that could be used for the casing of the games controller.

  .... [1]

  (ii) Give **three** reasons why thermoplastic polymers are suitable for the casing.

  1 ....

  .... [1]

  2 ....

  .... [1]

  3 ....

  .... [1]

(iii) Describe the process of making thermoplastic polymer from its raw material.

[4]

(b) The company is using anthropometric data to design the controller.

Give **two** pieces of anthropometric data that the designer would need to know in order to design the games controller. For each, describe how it would influence the design.

Data needed 1:

[1]

How it would influence the design:

[1]

Data needed 2:

[1]

How it would influence the design:

[1]

(c) The manufacturer has carried out a survey of potential customers. They were asked which colour they would prefer for the controller. The results are shown in Table 1.

Table 1

Colour	Preferred by (number)
Black	12
White	7
Yellow	5
Silver	5
Gold	9
No preference	6

(i) Use the information in Table 1 to create a bar chart showing the number of people who preferred each colour.

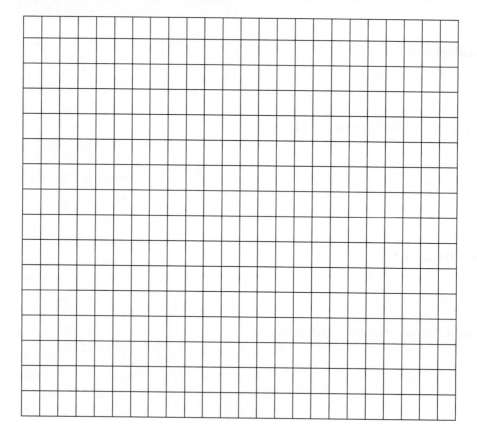

[4]

(ii) Calculate the percentage of people who had no preference for the colour.

[2]

(iii) Calculate the proportion of people who preferred black. Your answer should be expressed as a fraction.

[2]

(d) The company has calculated that each casing will contain 80 g of polymer.

It estimates that the process will produce waste of 2.5%.

Calculate the amount of material it should order to make a trial quantity of 6000 casings.

[3]

3 A designer has been tasked with designing a mobile phone charger that can be used when out camping.

Fig. 3 shows a mobile phone with a charger cable attached.

Fig. 3

(a) The designer is considering using solar panels to provide power for the product.

Circle the type of energy that solar panels provide.

Renewable   Non-renewable   [1]

(b) Give **two** advantages and **one** disadvantage of using solar panels to provide power for the product.

Advantage 1

....

.... [1]

Advantage 2

....

.... [1]

Disadvantage

....

.... [1]

(c) Give **two** ways of storing the energy collected by the solar panels.

1 .... [1]

2 .... [1]

(d) One of the solar panels will provide 900 milliamps of current. Convert this current value into amps.

....

....

....

....

.... [2]

(e) The designer wants the product to make a sound when the phone charging is complete.

Name **two** suitable electronic components that could be used for this purpose.

1 .... [1]

2 .... [1]

(f) Name **two** approaches that could be used to design the product. For each, explain **one** benefit of using it.

Design approach 1

.... [1]

Benefit

....

....

....

....

.... [2]

Design approach 2

.... [1]

Benefit

....

....

....

.... [2]

Section B

For all questions in Section B you must refer to the Insert. This contains images and information about products that you would find at an airport.

4   Refer to page 208 of the Insert.

(a)   The person in **Image A** is wearing a jacket made from natural fibres.

Give **three** reasons why natural fibres are suitable for this jacket.

1 _____ [1]

2 _____ [1]

3 _____ [1]

(b)   The person in **Image B** is wearing ear protection that uses foam to cover the ears.

Explain **two** reasons why foam is a suitable material for this application.

1 _____

_____

_____ [2]

2 _____

_____

_____ [2]

Practice Exam Paper

(c) The person in **Image C** is pulling a suitcase on wheels.

    (i) Name the type of motion that wheels produce.

    .... [1]

    (ii) Name **one** electronic output device that could make the wheels on the suitcase move automatically.

    .... [1]

(d) **Image D** shows a passenger jet aircraft made using composite materials.

Explain **two** reasons why composite materials are replacing aluminium alloys in aircraft.

1 ....

....

.... [2]

2 ....

....

.... [2]

You need to answer **questions 5 and 6** in relation to **one** of the products listed below covering an area you have studied in depth.

Information about the products is contained in the Insert.

Before you choose a product, read all parts of questions 5 and 6.

You **must** tick **one** box below to indicate your chosen product.

☐ Product 1: Gift Bag (Papers and Boards)

☐ Product 2: Pilots' Shirt (Fibres and Fabrics)

☐ Product 3: Automatic Car Park Barrier (Design Engineering)

☐ Product 4: Disposable Cup (Polymers)

☐ Product 5: Recycle Bin (Metals)

☐ Product 6: Café Chair (Timbers)

Practice Exam Paper

5   Study the images and technical information shown about your chosen product on the Insert.

(a)   Describe in detail how you would manufacture a **final prototype** of your chosen product in a school workshop.

Marks will be awarded for details of:

- The specific materials, components and manufacturing processes used to make the prototype.
- All tools and equipment used to both manufacture the product and ensure accuracy.
- The finishing techniques used.

....

....

....

....

....

....

....

....

....

....

....

....

....

[12]

Practice Exam Paper

(b) (i) Give **one** design method that ensures each different version of a prototype is evaluated and refined.

.... [1]

(ii) Explain **two** reasons why designers make prototypes.

1 ....

....

....

[2]

2 ....

....

....

[2]

(c)* Discuss the importance of considering usability when designing products for use in an airport environment.

Use the Insert to help you.

....

....

....

....

....

....

....

....

....

[9]

Practice Exam Paper

6   Use the same product you chose for Question 5 to answer this question.

It is important to consider the environment when selecting materials to use in products.

- Select a suitable material for your product based on its sustainability.
- Explain how this material choice would impact on the sustainability of the product.

Material chosen

Explanation

[6]

Collins

GCSE Design & Technology
GCSE (9–1) Design and Technology

Principles of Design and Technology

Insert

Time allowed: 2 hours

You must have:
• the Question Paper.

Information for Candidates

- This document is to be used when answering **Section B**.
- The images on page 208 are required to answer questions 4 and 5(c).
- The product information on pages 201–207 is required to answer questions 5 and 6.
- The question paper tells you when to refer to the information contained in this Insert.

Name: ....

Front view

Side view

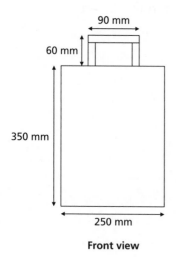

Front view

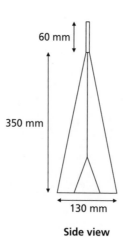

Side view

The bag is going to be batch produced. You need to consider the following needs for making the final prototype:

- How the design is laid out as a flat sheet prior to being made into a final bag.
- How the flat sheet is made into the final bag.
- How the bag that has been designed can be made so that it is recyclable.

Product 2: Pilots' Shirt (Fibres and Fabrics)

Front view   Back view   Side view

- The shoulder rank insignia patch is 90 mm × 40 mm.
- The shirt is to be made in the sizes shown in the table below.
- The final prototype of the shirt should be made to a large size.
- The shirt will be fastened using buttons.

	Extra Large	Large	Medium	Small
Neck to hip	690 mm	685 mm	675 mm	670 mm
Sleeve length	200 mm	200 mm	190 mm	190 mm
Chest size	1220 mm	1120 mm	1020 mm	920 mm
Neck size	440 mm	430 mm	420 mm	410 mm

Product 3: Automatic Car Park Barrier (Design Engineering)

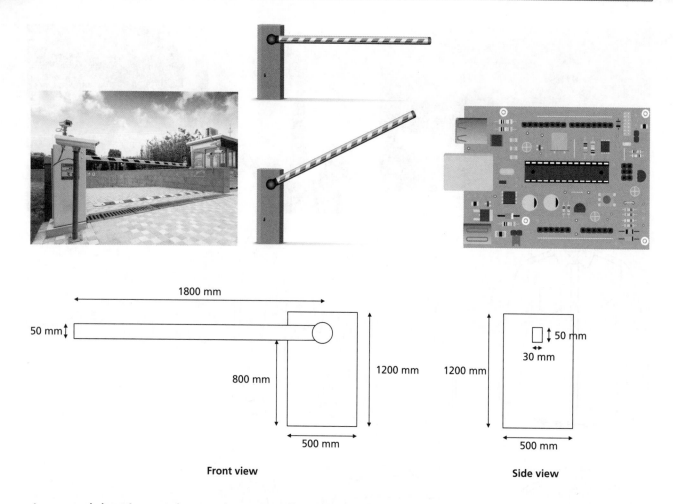

Front view

Side view

A car park barrier can be used to control access to the airport's car parking facilities. When a vehicle is detected at the barrier, the barrier opens. The barrier closes two seconds after the vehicle has passed through. This is controlled using a programmable device.

The final prototype should demonstrate to a stakeholder how the barrier functions. To do this you will need to use bought-in components, including a programmable device to control the opening and closing of the barrier. The prototype can be made as a scale model.

Product 4: Disposable Cup (Polymers)

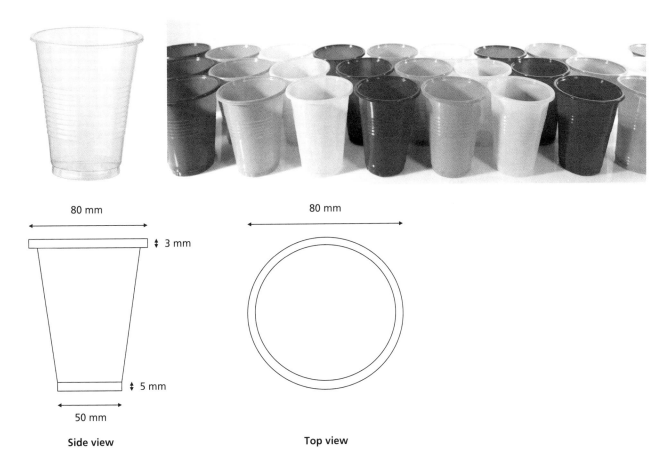

80 mm

3 mm

80 mm

5 mm

50 mm

Side view

Top view

The cup will be produced in large quantities. You need to consider the following needs for making the final prototype:

- The cup only needs to hold cold liquid. It does not need to hold hot liquid.
- Several cups should be stackable.
- The cup could be made in one of a range of different colours.

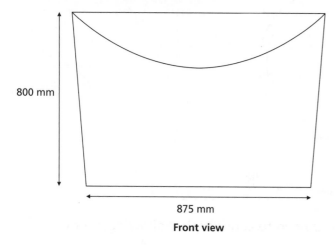

800 mm

875 mm

Front view

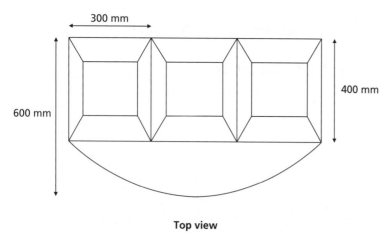

300 mm

600 mm

400 mm

Top view

Each bin will be produced using the same processes. It is designed to encourage greater recycling of waste in the airport departure terminal.

- The bin must be durable as it will be in constant use.
- It has three separate sections for inserting different types of waste: papers, plastics and general waste.

Product 6: Café Chair (Timbers)

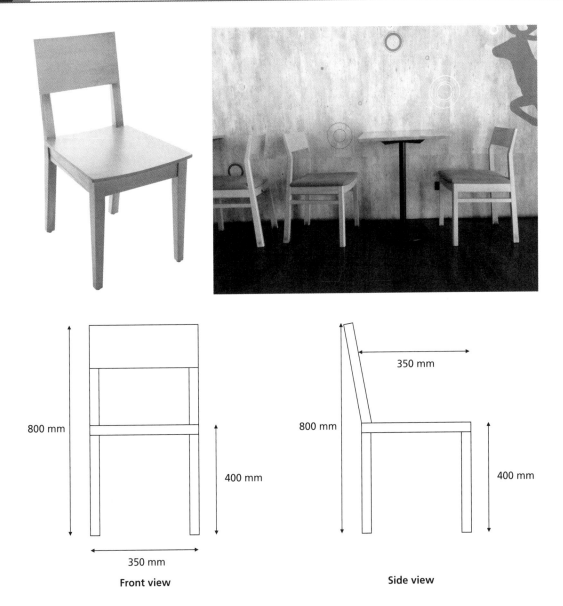

Front view

800 mm
400 mm
350 mm

Side view

800 mm
350 mm
400 mm

There are several chairs of the same shape, size and design used in cafés throughout the departure lounge of the airport. Some are cushioned for extra comfort.

- The chair is made from standard stock material. This is then cut and shaped.
- Suitable joining methods are used to attach the different sections of the chair together.
- The chair is strong but lightweight.

Practice Exam Paper Insert

Information on this page is required to answer questions 4 and 5(c).

Image A

Image B

Image C

Image D

Answers

Page 148 Exploring Context and Factors Affecting the Design Process

1. 1 mark for each suitable response. For example:
   - Where the product will be used [1]
   - How the product will be used [1]
   - User/stakeholder requirements [1]
   - Social factors [1]
   - Economic factors [1]
   - Social factors [1]
   - Moral factors [1]
2. Up to 2 marks for explanation of each reason. For example: to discuss the client's requirements [1] to ensure that they are considered during the design process [1]. To share initial thoughts about potential solutions [1] so that feedback can be gathered [1].

Page 149 Usability

1. 7–9 marks: thorough knowledge and understanding of the importance of using anthropometric data when designing products. Balanced discussion that comes to an appropriate, qualified conclusion. Several relevant examples presented to support answer. 4–6 marks: good knowledge and understanding of importance of using anthropometric data when designing products. Some balance to the discussion. Conclusion made but may not be qualified. Some relevant examples presented to support answer. 1–3 marks: limited knowledge or understanding. Mainly descriptive response and lack of balance. No conclusion. Few or no relevant examples presented to support answer.
   Indicative answer: Products need to be designed so that they are ergonomic. Anthropometric data is measurements taken from millions of people and placed in charts that can be used by designers to ensure products fit the human body and/or are easy to interact with. For example, when designing a chair the sitting heights should be considered when deciding how high the legs should be; shoulder breadth would determine the width of the chair. If anthropometric data is not used products may not fit the intended user. For example, if head circumferences are not considered when designing a hat, it may end up too big or too small for the user. The fifth to 95th percentile can be used to ensure 90% of the population are catered for.

Page 150 Exploring Existing Designs

1. 1 mark for each suitable response. For example:
   - Materials/components/processes that have been used [1]
   - Influence of trends/fashion/taste/style [1]
   - Influence of marketing/branding [1]
   - The impact on society [1]
   - The impact on usability [1]
   - Impact on environment/sustainability [1]
   - Comparison to past designs [1]
2. Systematically evaluating the environmental aspects of a product or system [1].

Page 151 New and Emerging Technologies

1. 1 mark for any appropriate new and emerging technology and up to 2 marks for explanation. For example: bioplastics [1]. These could be used to replace plastic carrier bags [1], therefore reducing the amount of oil that needs to be sourced [1].
2. 1 mark for any appropriate new and emerging technology and up to 2 marks for explanation. For example: nanotechnology [1]. This could be used to improve healthcare [1] by improving the delivery of medicines within the body [1].

Page 152 Sources of Energy

1. 1 mark for stating whether each source of energy is renewable or non-renewable and up to 2 marks for suitable description of how each is used to produce energy. For example:

Source of Energy	Renewable or Non-Renewable	Description of How Energy is Produced
Nuclear fuel	Non-renewable [1]	A nuclear reactor creates steam [1] that is used to turn turbines [1]. *Reference must be made to nuclear reactor or nuclear reaction producing steam to gain 1 mark.*
Solar energy	Renewable [1]	Solar panels collect light from the sun [1] and convert it into an electric current [1].
Wind energy	Renewable [1]	The wind turns turbines [1] that then drive generators to produce electricity [1].

Page 153 Wider Influences on Designing and Making

1. Up to 2 marks for explanation of each way. For example: choose recyclable materials [1] so that less new material needs to be sourced [1]. Design for disassembly [1] so that materials/components can be reused [1]. Select a sustainable power supply [1] to reduce reliance on non-renewable energy [1].
2. Up to 2 marks for definition. For example: fair trade is a movement that works to help people in developing countries [1] to get a fair deal for the products that they produce [1].
3. Designing with regard to people's principles, beliefs and culture [1].

Page 154 Viability of Design Solutions

1. Up to 2 marks for definition. For example: the ability of a product to grow after initial sales [1] because of recommendations [1].
2. 5–6 marks: thorough knowledge and understanding of the factors that affect the commercial viability of a product. Balanced discussion. 3–4 marks: good knowledge and understanding of the factors that affect the commercial viability of a product. Some balance to the discussion. 1–2 marks: limited knowledge or understanding. Mainly descriptive response and lack of balance.
   Indicative answer: Commercial products must make a profit when sold. There must be a suitable target market for the product. This must be identified, often through market research or by analysing the success of products made by competitors. If there is no market for a product it will not sell well. Being first to market can have a hugely positive impact on sales/can result in the product becoming the market leader, whereas being last may mean the market has already become saturated. No amount of marketing will be able to sell a poor product that does not do its job, so the product must be of the required quality. The selling price will affect how well a product sells. This will be determined by the cost of production, including the quality of materials and components used.

Page 155 Graphical Techniques 1

1. 1 mark for a 3D sketch that shows a suitable design for the table.
   1 mark for suitable material(s) chosen and 1 mark for reason why. For example: ABS (acrylonitrile butadiene) [1] because it has good toughness [1].
   1 mark for suitable manufacturing process(s) chosen and 1 mark for suitable reason why. For example: injection moulding [1] as it produces a very strong product [1].

Page 156 Graphical Techniques 2

1. a) To show the order in which a series of commands or events are carried out [1].
   b) Up to 2 marks for explanation of each benefit. For example: it provides a clear representation of the steps needed to manufacture the product [1], making them easier to communicate to other people [1]. It shows the exact order of operations needed to manufacture the product [1], making it easier to ensure the right equipment is available at the right time [1].
2. Up to 2 marks for explanation of each reason. For example: to assist with manufacture/assembly [1] as it shows how all the parts will fit together [1]. To explain the details of the idea to a client [1] as it shows each individual part clearly [1].

Page 157 Approaches to Designing

1. 1 mark for each suitable response. For example:

Design Approach	Advantage of Approach	Disadvantage of Approach
Iterative design	Problems with the design can be discovered and dealt with earlier [1].	It can be time consuming if a lot of prototypes or iterations need to be produced [1].
User-centred design	The end user has a greater ownership of the final product [1].	The design could become too focused on one particular end user's requirements [1].
Systems thinking	It is easier to find errors or faults in the design [1].	It can lead to the use of components that are not necessary [1].

Page 158 Properties of Materials

1. a) The ability of a material not to break when a force is applied to it suddenly [1]
   b) The ability of electricity to pass through a material [1]

c) The ability of a material to return to its original shape when a force is removed [1]
2. a) Corrosion resistance [1]
   b) Strength to weight ratio [1]
   c) Absorbency [1]
3. A physical property is a measurable characteristic of the material itself [1] whereas a mechanical property is a reaction to some form of applied force [1].

Page 159 Factors Influencing Material Selection

1. a) How well the product carries out the task that it was designed to do [1]
   b) How an object appeals to the five senses [1]
2. Award marks as indicated, up to a maximum of 6 marks. Whether the material is renewable/naturally replenished within a short time/made from finite resources [1] Whether the environment is damaged to obtain/extract the material [1] The amount (and impact) of transportation needed for the material [1] The amount of waste created when using the material [1] What happens to the product at the end of its usable life [1]; whether it is incinerated/goes to landfill [1] or can be recycled [1] Any other relevant point [1].

Page 160 Paper and Board

1. Award up to 4 marks as follows: bleached card is made from pure bleached wood pulp [1] and is white all the way through [1]. Carton board has white surfaces with grey fibres in between [1] and costs less than bleached card [1]. It also has slightly less strength [1]. The available thicknesses of carton board are typically slightly greater than for bleached card [1].
2. Award 1 mark for an attempt to tessellate that is inefficient. Award 2 marks for effective tessellation. For example:

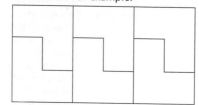

Page 161 Timber

1. Award up to 4 marks as follows, for information shown in either sketches or presented as notes: both are manufactured using layers of veneers positioned at 90° to each other [1]. In plywood these layers are through the full thickness of the material whereas in blockboard there is a central core of strips of timber [1]. This means the

properties of plywood are uniform in the x and y directions [1], whereas blockboard is stronger in the direction in which the strips are oriented [1].
2. Award marks as indicated, up to a maximum of 6 marks. Hardwood grows slowly, so cannot quickly be replaced [1]. It is cut from the tree as planks, which leaves a significant quantity of waste or unused material [1]. MDF can be made from either hardwood or softwood [1] and almost all the material is used/there is very little waste [1]. During its working life, oak is stronger and harder, so likely to last longer than MDF [1], reducing the need for replacement materials [1]. At the end of its usable life, MDF will normally either be incinerated or go to landfill [1], whereas oak could be incinerated (for fuel), but could also be broken down into particles to make MDF [1]. Any other relevant point [1].

Page 162 Metals

1. a) Award 1 mark each for iron and chromium.
   b) Award 1 mark each for tin and lead.
   c) Award 1 mark each for up to two of tin, copper and antimony.
   d) Award 1 mark each for copper and zinc.
2. a) Award 1 mark each for up to four of the following: sheet, plate, round bar, square bar, square tube and round tube.
   b) Award marks as indicated, up to a maximum of 4 marks: to reform metal it requires much energy [1] and effort [1], and therefore cost [1]. By using a stock form, this cost can be avoided [1].

Page 163 Polymers

1. Award marks as indicated up to a maximum of 4 marks, for notes or sketches communicating the following content: oil is extracted [1]; this is sent to an industrial refinery [1]; small chemical units called monomers are extracted from the oil [1], which are linked together to form the polymer chains in the polymerisation process [1]. This material can then be extruded/rolled/granulated into the required form [1].
2. Volume of 1 cube = 0.03^3 [1] = 2.7×10^{-5} m³ [1]
   Volume of 10 000 cubes = $2.7 \times 10^{-5} \times$ 10 000 = 0.27 m³ [1]
   Mass of 10 000 cubes = 0.27×960 [1] = 259.2 kg [1]

Page 164 Textiles

1. a) Award 1 mark for cotton, wool or silk.
   b) Award 1 mark for a suitable application. For example: underwear, shirts and blouses,

T-shirts or jeans for cotton; jumpers, suits, dresses or carpets for wool; dresses, shirts or ties for silk.

c) Award 1 mark each for up to three properties that make it suitable for the stated application. For example: strong, durable and absorbent for cotton; warm, soft, absorbent and crease resistant for wool; smooth, lustrous and strong for silk.

2. a) Award 1 mark for polyamide/nylon, polyester or acrylic.
   b) Award 1 mark for a suitable application. For example: tights and stockings, sportswear, upholstery, carpets for nylon; sportswear for polyester; clothing, fake fur, furnishings for acrylic.
   c) Award 1 mark each for up to three properties that make it suitable for the stated application. For example: strong, durable, warm and crease resistant for nylon; strong, durable, elastic and crease resistant for polyester; soft, warm and similar to wool for acrylic.

Page 165 New Developments in Materials

1. a) Award 1 mark for a named composite, for example glass-reinforced polyester (GRP), fibreglass, carbon-reinforced polyester (CRP) or reinforced concrete.
   b) Award 1 mark for a suitable application for the composite stated in (a). For example: car bodies or boat hulls for GRP and fibreglass; tent poles or high-performance bicycles for CRP; buildings for reinforced concrete.

2. Superalloys are used in preference to other metals; they have excellent strength [1], corrosion resistance [1] and resistance to creep [1].

3. Award marks as indicated, up to a maximum of 4 marks: biopolymers are polymers produced by living organisms [1]. Synthetic polymers are made from fossil fuels such as oil [1], a finite resource [1]. Unlike synthetic polymers, biopolymers are biodegradable [1], carbon-neutral [1], renewable [1] and suitable to be composted [1].
Any other relevant point.

Page 166 Standard Components

1. a) Award 1 mark each for any two of: clips, fasteners, bindings.
   b) Award 1 mark each for any two of: zips, buttons, press studs, velcro, decorative items.
   c) Award 1 mark each for any two of: nuts and bolts, rivets, hinges.
   d) Award 1 mark each for any two of: hinges, brackets, screws, nails.

2. Award marks as indicated, up to a maximum of 4 marks: making components in small quantities can be very expensive [1] due to the labour time [1] and equipment required [1]. It normally costs less to buy standard components [1] and more consistent quality can be offered [1].
Any other relevant point [1].

Page 167 Finishing Materials

1. 1 mark for each suitable finishing technique for each material. For example:

Type of Material	Finishing Technique 1	Finishing Technique 2
Paper and board	Laminating [1]	Embossing [1]
Timber	Varnishing [1]	Oiling [1]
Metal	Anodising [1]	Plating [1]
Polymer/plastic	Polishing [1]	Self-finishing [1]
Fibres and fabrics	Brushing [1]	Bleaching [1]

Page 168 Structural Integrity

1. Award marks as indicated up to a maximum of 4 marks: use a stronger material [1]; increase the wall thickness [1]; add ribs to the outside [1] or add webbing to the inside of the casing [1], all of which increase the rigidity of the casing [1].

2. a) Interfacing means adding extra materials to a textile product [1] to increase its strength or make it more rigid [1].
   b) 1 mark for a suitable example, for example shirt collars or behind button holes.

Page 169 Motion and Levers

1. a) Oscillating [1]
   b) Linear [1]
   c) Rotating [1]
   d) Reciprocating [1]

2. Mechanical advantage = load / effort [1] = 60 / 24 = 2.5 [1]
For a first-class lever, as mechanical advantage = A / 60,
rearranging A = mechanical advantage × 60 [1] = 2.5 × 60 = 150 mm [1]

Page 170 Mechanical Devices

1. Award marks for notes or sketches communicating the following content. A follower can only rise (go up), dwell (be held at the same height) or fall (go down) [1]. How long the follower spends doing each of these depends on the shape of the cam [1]. A round section on the cam will provide a dwell [1]. The longer the round section, the longer the dwell [1]. A snail cam (or similar) will provide a sudden drop [1]. Any other relevant point [1].

2. Gear ratio needed = speed of output gear / speed of input gear [1] = 240 / 60 = 4:1 [1]
Number of teeth needed = number of teeth on input gear / gear ratio [1] = 48 / 4 = 12 [1]

Page 171 Electronic Systems

1. 1 mark for stating whether each component is an input or output and 1 mark for suitable application of each. For example:

Component	Input or Output	Application
Push switch	Input [1]	Starting the timing sequence on a kitchen timer [1]
Light-emitting diode (LED)	Output [1]	Providing light for a bicycle safety lamp [1]
Motor	Output [1]	Turning the blades on a handheld fan [1]
Light-dependent resistor (LDR)	Input [1]	Light sensor for a garden light that comes on when it is dark [1]
Buzzer	Output [1]	Making a buzzing sound for a doorbell [1]

Page 172 Programmable Components

1. 1 mark for showing how/where the program starts and ends, 1 mark for a way of checking the sensor, 1 mark for turning the light on after the sensor has detected movement, 1 mark for way of setting the correct time period, 1 mark for turning the light off.
Any appropriate programming language may be used, including raw code or block- or flow-chart-based approaches.

Page 173 Modelling Processes

1. 5–6 marks: detailed and thorough description of the technique. All tools and equipment needed are included. Detailed supporting sketches for every stage of the process. 3–4 marks: good description of the technique. Most tools and equipment needed are included. Some supporting sketches showing some detail. 1–2 marks: basic description of the technique. A few tools and equipment needed are included. A few basic supporting sketches.
For example, for producing a card model steps could include: Measure and mark out the card pieces required using a pencil, a ruler, a protractor, etc. Use scissors, a craft knife (with safety rule/protective mat) and/or a rotary trimmer to cut the card pieces to shape. Assemble the card pieces together using a glue gun, masking/double-sided tape or other suitable tapes/adhesives.

Page 174 Wastage

1. a) Award 1 mark for tenon saw.
   b) Award 1 mark for cutting circles.
   c) Award 1 mark for metal.
   d) Award 1 mark for paper and card.
   e) Award 1 mark for cutting straight lines.
   f) Award 1 mark for pinking shears.
   g) Award 1 mark for centre lathe.

Page 175 Additive Manufacturing Processes

1. Award marks as indicated up to a maximum of 6 marks: the parts to be joined are cleaned [1] and any oxide, rust or grease is removed [1]. They are placed together to form the joint [1]. A heat source from a flame/electric arc is applied [1]. This melts the edges of the parts so they join together [1]. A filler wire may be used [1] especially if there is a gap between the parts being joined [1]. The joint is then allowed to cool [1] and cleaned/descaled if necessary [1].

2. Award marks as indicated up to a maximum of 4 marks. Brazing is carried out at a lower temperature than welding [1]. The parts to be joined do not melt [1]. A filler metal must be used: in welding this is sometimes not needed [1]. The joint is a different alloy to the parent metal [1]. A brazed joint is not normally as strong as a welded joint [1]. Any other relevant point [1].

3. Award one mark for either epoxy resin or riveting.

Page 176 Deforming and Reforming

1. Award marks as follows up to a maximum of 10 marks (information can be conveyed in either sketches or notes). A mould is made [1]. The mould is placed inside the vacuum-forming machine [1]. A sheet of material is clamped across the top [1]. The material must be a thermoplastic polymer [1]. The material is heated until it softens [1]. The mould is raised [1]. A vacuum is applied to suck out the air between the mould and the plastic [1]. Air pressure from the atmosphere pushes the plastic against the mould [1]. Air may be blown in to help the mould release from the product [1]. The mould is lowered and the plastic sheet is unclamped [1]. The product is cut out of the plastic sheet [1].

Page 177 Ensuring Accuracy

1. Up to 2 marks for explanation of reason. For example: a small deviation from dimensions given in the specification [1] can result in a product that is not fit for purpose [1].

2. Up to 2 marks for explanation of each example. For example: jig: holding and positioning a drill [1] to ensure that holes are drilled in the same place on two pieces of wood [1]. Pattern: providing a pattern for a dress [1] so that the parts can be traced accurately onto fabric [1].

Page 178 Digital Design Tools

1. 1 mark for each suitable response. For example: when preparing images of product prototypes for a presentation to stakeholders [1]. When designing a pictorial logo to go on product packaging [1].

2. 1 mark for correct definition. For example: approach to manufacturing that is centred around a computer system [1].

3. 1 mark for correct definition. For example: processes used to quickly produce a product or component directly from computer-aided design (CAD) data [1].

4. Up to 2 marks for explanation of benefit. For example: the prototype created can be fully evaluated [1] so errors in the design can be found before the final product is manufactured [1].

Page 179 Scales of Manufacture

1. a) Award marks as indicated: a group of identical products are made together [1], followed by other groups of similar (but not necessarily identical) products [1].
   b) Award 1 mark each for two suitable examples. For example: chairs, clothes for high-street stores.

2. Award marks as indicated up to a maximum of 8 marks. Lean manufacturing aims to eliminate waste during manufacturing [1]. Waste refers to any activity that does not add value to the product [1]. Eliminating waste normally reduces the cost required to make the product in some way [1]. There are many types of waste:
   • Time looking for tools [1], as this takes operator time which costs money [1]. This can be reduced by using tool boards [1].
   • Moving products around a factory [1]. This can be reduced by using conveyors/automation to move products [1] or reducing distances between processes [1].
   • Making too many products [1], as this ties up money in stock [1].
   • Doing more to the product than the customer needs [1], as this overprocessing [1] takes labour time [1] or can even involve buying more expensive machines than needed [1].
   • Making defective parts [1] due to the cost of material [1] and the labour cost spent on making the product being lost [1].
   • Any other relevant point [1].

Page 180 Large-Scale Processes: Paper, Timber and Metals

1. Award marks as follows up to a maximum of 5 marks (information can be conveyed in either sketches or notes):
   • The image to print is in relief on the printing plate [1].
   • Ink is applied, which is attracted to the image [1].
   • The plate is dampened, which repels ink of any non-image areas [1].
   • The printing plate transfers an inked image onto the rubber blanket cylinder [1].
   • The rubber blanket cylinder presses the image onto the paper or card as it is fed through [1].

2. Award marks as indicated up to a maximum of 4 marks: die casting uses a reusable metal mould [1] which is much more expensive than a mould made from sand [1]. Even though in sand casting a new mould has to be made every time [1], for a batch of 10 products the total cost will probably be less than the cost of the metal mould [1]. Further, the equipment cost for sand casting is much less than for die casting [1].

Page 181 Large-Scale Processes: Polymers and Fabrics

1. Award marks as indicated up to a maximum of 4 marks. A maximum of 2 marks can be achieved if only advantages or disadvantages are stated:
   • Advantage: rapid prototyping can produce a prototype much faster than conventional machining [1].
   • Advantage: the prototype can be produced directly from a CAD model [1].
   • Disadvantage: the mechanical properties of the rapid prototype may be different from the final product [1] as it may use different materials to those that the final product would be made from [1].
   • Disadvantage: the design may have features that cannot subsequently be manufactured using conventional processes [1].
   • Any other relevant point [1].

2. Award marks as follows up to a maximum of 5 marks (information can be conveyed in either sketches or notes). Plastic powder or granules are fed from a hopper into the machine [1]. Heaters melt the plastic [1]. A screw moves the plastic along towards the mould [1]. The screw provides pressure on the plastic turning it into a continuous stream [1]. The pressure forces the plastic through a die in the profile of the tube, creating the pipe [1].

Pages 182–192 Practice Exam Paper
Section A

1. (a) Up to 2 marks for explanation of each factor. For example:
    - The impact of current fashion/ trends on the design [1], as a design that is not fashionable may not sell well [1].
    - Its potential impact on the environment [1] as a product that makes use of recyclable materials would be more sustainable [1].
    - How it compares to past designs [1] as customers would expect to see improvements from previous versions of the product [1].
   (b) Up to 2 marks for calculation. For example:
    £40 – £25 = £15 [1]
    15/40 = 0.375; 0.375 x 100 = 37.5% [1]
   (c) Up to 2 marks for explanation of each reason. For example:
    - It allows the ideas to be drawn quickly [1] as formal drawing standards do not need to be followed [1].
    - To keep the client focused on the general concept [1] as exact details do not need to be included [1].
   (d) Up to 2 marks for explanation of each benefit. For example:
    - It can convert hand drawings into 3D models [1], which saves time drawing them again in CAD software [1].
    - Any designer can use it with very little training [1] as it does not require specialist knowledge of using 3D modelling programs [1].

2. (a) (i) One from:
    - polypropylene (PP)
    - acrylonitrile butadiene styrene (ABS)
    - high-density polyethylene (HDPE)
    - low-density polyethylene (LDPE)
    - polyvinylchloride (PVC).
   (ii) Three from:
    - insulator
    - waterproof
    - tough/durable
    - lightweight
    - easy to mould
    - available in bright colours
    - easy to clean.
   (iii) Award up to four marks as indicated:
    - Oil is extracted by drilling [1].
    - This is sent to an industrial refinery [1].
    - Small chemical units called monomers are extracted from the oil [1].
    - These are linked together to form the polymer chains in the polymerisation process [1].
    - This material can then be extruded/rolled/granulated into the required form [1].

   (b) Award marks as indicated. Two from:
    - Finger diameter [1] determines button size [1].
    - Thumb length [1] determines position of controls [1].
    - Grip diameter [1] determines diameter of held section [1].
    - Award credit for any other appropriate response.
   (c) (i) Award 1 mark each for correct selection of x (colour preference) and y (number of people) axes. Award 1 mark if at least one of the bars is at the correct value, and 2 marks if all the bars are the correct values.
       (ii) Total number of people = 40 [1]
        Percentage = 6/40 × 100/1 = 15% [1]
       (iii) 12/40 [1] = 3/10 [1]
   (d) Weight of polymer needed per casing including waste = 80 g × 1.025 [1] = 82 g [1]
    Total weight of polymer needed = 6000 × 82 g = 492 000 g = 492 kg [1]

3. (a) 1 mark for circling the word renewable.
   (b) Up to 2 marks for advantages and 1 mark for disadvantage. For example:
    - Advantages: solar panels have zero greenhouse/carbon emissions [1]; solar energy will not run out in our lifetime [1].
    - Disadvantage: solar panels cannot collect energy at night [1].
   (c) 1 mark for each suitable method up to a maximum of 2 marks, such as battery [1], fuel cell [1] or supercapacitor [1].
   (d) Up to 2 marks for conversion. For example:
    900/1000 [1] = 0.9 A [1]
   (e) 1 mark each for buzzer [1] and speaker [1].
   (f) 1 mark for each suitable approach. Up to 2 marks for explanation of each benefit. For example:
    - User-centred design [1]. There would be constant user feedback [1], which would result in a product that matches their needs better [1].
    - Systems approach [1]. This would provide a top-down overview of the system design [1], which would make it easier to explain to stakeholders [1].

Pages 193–200 Practice Exam Paper
Section B

4. (a) 1 mark for each suitable reason. For example:
    - They are comfortable to wear [1]
    - Easy to dye/good dye absorbency [1]
    - Good thermal properties [1].
   (b) Up to 2 marks for explanation of each reason. For example:

    - It has good sound-deadening properties [1], which would protect the wearer from ear damage caused by loud aircraft engines [1].
    - It is soft/flexible [1] and so would be comfortable to wear for long periods [1].
   (c) 1 mark for each correct answer.
    (i) Rotary [1]
    (ii) Motor [1]
   (d) Up to 2 marks for explanation of each reason. For example:
    - Composites are more lightweight [1], which would reduce the amount fuel needed by the aircraft [1].
    - Composites do not to corrode [1], resulting in less likelihood of crashes/accidents [1].

5. (a) 9–12 marks: information on the Insert has been fully analysed. Comprehensive and well-planned response containing an excellent description of the making process. Thorough knowledge of the appropriate materials, components, tools, equipment, processes and finishing techniques needed to make the prototype and ensure accuracy. Excellent use of specialist terminology. 5–8 marks: information on the Insert has been analysed adequately. Good response that shows some evidence of planning and contains a good description of the making process. Good and mainly appropriate knowledge of the appropriate materials, components, tools, equipment, processes and finishing techniques needed to make the prototype and ensure accuracy. Good use of specialist terminology, but some may not be appropriate. 1–4 marks: limited analysis of the information presented on the Insert. Limited response that shows a basic understanding of the making process. Basic knowledge of the appropriate materials, components, tools, equipment, processes and finishing techniques needed to make the prototype and ensure accuracy, some of which may be inappropriate. Limited and sometime inappropriate use of specialist terminology.
    Indicative content; for example: for Product 4 (polymers):
    - Materials: high-impact polystyrene (HIPS), polyethylene terephthalate (PET).
    - Processes/techniques/skills: making moulds, vacuum forming, injection moulding or other appropriate forming/moulding techniques, rapid prototyping.
    - Tools: saws/cutting tools, drills, files, vacuum former, injection moulding machine/injection press, 3D printer.

- Accuracy: jigs, moulds, templates.
- Finishing: using self-finishing polymers, smart colours/pigments.

(b) (i) 1 mark for iterative design **[1]**.

(ii) Up to 2 marks for explanation of each reason. For example: it allows stakeholders to evaluate the prototype **[1]**, which results in improvements to the next iteration **[1]**. It helps with the identification of a unique selling point (USP) **[1]** which would make it more marketable **[1]**.

(c) All responses should be in the context of an airport environment. 7–9 marks: thorough knowledge and understanding of the importance of considering usability when designing products for use in an airport environment. Balanced discussion that comes to an appropriate, qualified conclusion. 4–6 marks: good knowledge and understanding of the importance of considering usability when designing products for use in an airport environment. Some balance to the discussion. Conclusion made but may not be qualified. 1–3 marks: limited knowledge or understanding. Mainly descriptive response and lack of balance. No conclusion.

Indicative content:
- Inclusivity/ease of use: information text on displays of suitable size so that people with sight problems can see it.
- Information and desks (ticket collection, passport control, etc.) of height that can be accessed by people in wheelchairs.
- Suitable use of escalators, lifts, support vehicles, etc., for people who have difficulty getting up and down stairs, accessing the aircraft from the terminal building or moving long distances/moving luggage within the airport.
- Ergonomics/anthropometrics: use of anthropometric data for the design of products, such as leg length for chairs, finger/hand size for using buttons on car park ticket dispensers, etc. Use of ergonomics to ensure comfortable seating in terminal and on aircraft.
- Aesthetics: use of attractive and informative colour schemes on signage, use of calming colours/avoiding aggressive colours in terminal building to reduce stress.

6. 5–6 marks: thorough knowledge and understanding of how the material chosen would impact on the sustainability of the product. All points fully explained. 3–4 marks: good knowledge and understanding of how the material chosen would impact on the sustainability of the product. Majority of points explained. 1–2 marks: limited knowledge or understanding. Mainly descriptive response.

Indicative content; for example: for Product 4 (polymers):
- Use bioplastics instead of traditional oil-based plastics.
- This would result in less oil needing to be drilled for, thus reducing carbon emissions and reliance on fossil fuels.
- Bioplastics are biodegradable, thus reducing the amount of landfill waste produced.
- Traditional plastics can take thousands of years to degrade and cause damage and death to wildlife over a long period of time.

Revision Tips

Rethink Revision

Have you ever taken part in a quiz and thought '*I know this*!', but, despite frantically racking your brain, you just couldn't come up with the answer?

It's very frustrating when this happens, but in a fun situation it doesn't really matter. However, in your GCSE exams, it will be essential that you can recall the relevant information quickly when you need to.

Most students think that revision is about making sure you *know* stuff. Of course, this is important, but it is also about becoming confident that you can **retain** that *stuff* over time and **recall** it quickly when needed.

Revision That Really Works

Experts have discovered that there are two techniques that help with all of these things and consistently produce better results in exams compared to other revision techniques.

Applying these techniques to your GCSE revision will ensure you get better results in your exams and will have all the relevant knowledge at your fingertips when you start studying for further qualifications, like AS and A Levels, or begin work.

It really isn't rocket science either – you simply need to:

- **test yourself** on each topic as many times as possible
- **leave a gap** between the test sessions.

It is most effective if you leave a good period of time between the test sessions, e.g. between a week and a month. The idea is that just as you start to forget the information, you force yourself to recall it again, keeping it fresh in your mind.

Three Essential Revision Tips

1. **Use Your Time Wisely**
   - Allow yourself plenty of time.
   - Try to start revising six months before your exams – it's more effective and less stressful.
   - Your revision time is precious so use it wisely – using the techniques described on this page will ensure you revise effectively and efficiently and get the best results.
   - Don't waste time re-reading the same information over and over again – it's time-consuming and not effective!

2. **Make a Plan**
   - Identify all the topics you need to revise (this All-in-One Revision & Practice book will help you).
   - Plan at least five sessions for each topic.
   - One hour should be ample time to test yourself on the key ideas for a topic.
   - Spread out the practice sessions for each topic – the optimum time to leave between each session is about one month but, if this isn't possible, just make the gaps as big as realistically possible.

3. **Test Yourself**
   - Methods for testing yourself include: quizzes, practice questions, flashcards, past papers, explaining a topic to someone else, etc.
   - This All-in-One Revision & Practice book provides seven practice opportunities per topic.
   - Don't worry if you get an answer wrong – provided you check what the correct answer is, you are more likely to get the same or similar questions right in future!

Visit our website to download your free flashcards, for more information about the benefits of these revision techniques, and for further guidance on how to plan ahead and make them work for you.

www.collins.co.uk/collinsGCSErevision

Collins GCSE 9-1 Revision

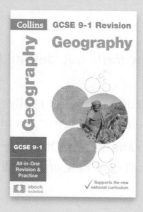

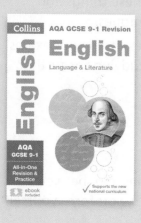

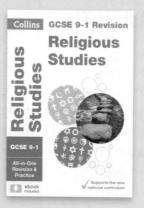

Visit the website to view the complete range and place an order:

www.collins.co.uk/collinsGCSErevision

ACKNOWLEDGEMENTS

The author and publisher are grateful to the copyright holders for permission to use quoted materials and images.

Cover, p.1, p.145 © violetblue/Shutterstock.com
p.11 © David Gee 1 / Alamy Stock Photo
p.103 © www.optitex.com
All other images © Shutterstock.com

Every effort has been made to trace copyright holders and obtain their permission for the use of copyright material. The author and publisher will gladly receive information enabling them to rectify any error or omission in subsequent editions. All facts are correct at time of going to press.

Published by Collins
An imprint of HarperCollinsPublishers Ltd
1 London Bridge Street
London SE1 9GF

© HarperCollinsPublishers Limited 2017

ISBN 9780008227418

First published 2017

10 9 8 7 6 5 4 3

British Library Cataloguing in Publication Data.

A CIP record of this book is available from the British Library.

Authored by: Paul Anderson and David Hills-Taylor
Project management and editorial: Nik Prowse
Commissioning: Katherine Wilkinson and Katie Galloway
Cover Design: Sarah Duxbury and Paul Oates
Inside Concept Design: Sarah Duxbury and Paul Oates
Text Design and Layout: Jouve India Private Limited
Production: Natalia Rebow
Printed and bound in China by RR Donnelley APS

MIX
Paper from
responsible source
FSC C007454

This book is produced from independently certified FSC™ paper to ensure responsible forest management.

For more information visit:
www.harpercollins.co.uk/green

6 EASY WAYS TO ORDER

1. Available from collins.co.uk
2. Fax your order to 01484 665736
3. Phone us on 01484 668148
4. Email us at education@harpercollins.co.uk
5. Post your order to: Collins Education, FREEPOST RTKB-SGZT-ZYJL, Honley HD9 6QZ
6. Or visit your local bookshop.